T0295927

Rural Marketing as a Tool for National Development

Rural Marketing as a Tool for National Development: Strategies for Socio-Economic Progress

BY

CHARLES CHATTERJEE

Global Policy Institute, UK

United Kingdom – North America – Japan – India – Malaysia – China

Emerald Publishing Limited
Emerald Publishing, Floor 5, Northspring, 21-23 Wellington Street, Leeds LS1 4DL

First edition 2024

Reprints and permissions service
Contact: www.copyright.com

British Library Cataloguing in Publication Data
A catalogue record for this book is available from the British Library

ISBN: 978-1-83608-065-7 (Print)
ISBN: 978-1-83608-064-0 (Online)
ISBN: 978-1-83608-066-4 (Epub)

INVESTOR IN PEOPLE

Contents

About the Author

Professor Charles Chatterjee studied law at the University of Cambridge and the University of London. He held a professorial position in international commercial and criminal law at London Metropolitan University. He was a Senior Associate Fellow at University of Warwick, and until recently, he was also the Director of the Centre for Energy Law and Management at a British University. He is currently a Senior Research Fellow at the Global Policy Institute in addition to being a Visiting Professor at the National University of the Oriental Republic of Uruguay.

Professor Chatterjee is also a practising Barrister in England and Wales.

He has published extensively both in the form of books and articles on various aspects of public international law, international economic law, energy law, international commercial law, including banking, trade, investment, corporate governance, international commercial arbitration as well as health and drugs law.

Introduction

A number of books have already been published, on rural development, but, unfortunately, the vast majority of these publications have actually addressed the issue of 'rural marketing' procedures without even thoroughly examining the issue of whether the rural marketing procedures, which the experts in marketing recommend, would be applicable to the rural markets in the developing countries, bearing in mind that most of the essential factors for rural marketing, namely, publicity of products, the contribution of the climate at different times of the year and the capacity to purchase the products, often presents circumstantial hindrances, which need special efforts from united inhabitants in the areas concerned.[1] For example, in many parts of the developing countries, there appears strategies of water supply for meeting the requirements of irrigation, such as India has been facilitating irrigation for the crop-producing lands, especially during the summer months by preserving water in special reservoirs. These supplementary means, at least initially, prove to be indispensable.

Rural people, in general, in the developing countries, are frustrated in view of what may be described as an almost total neglect of the rural areas, even though by referring to their zeal and enthusiasm one may surmise what might have happened if they had received part of the development received by the non-rural areas.

It is for the indigenous people to push their governments to transform rural areas in order to make a country more useful by setting up new industries, education centres and catering for training centres. Leaving vast areas of land in a country without any purposeful development will not give any benefit to that country.

Rural areas may also form the platforms for socio-economic development in a country, but unfortunately, most of the developing countries seem to have ignored these areas; instead, they have prioritised their urban areas for 'development', which effectively was perceived to be a form of Westernisation. This work

---

[1]See P V Baran, 'The Political Economy of Growth', New York, *Monthly Review Press* (1957); R Chambers, *Rural Development: Putting the Last First*, Harlow, Prentice Hall (1983); W Easterly, *The Tyranny of Experts: Economists, Dictators and the Forgotten Rights of the Poor*, New York, Basic Books (2013).

Rural Marketing as a Tool for National Development, 1–2
Copyright © 2024 Charles Chatterjee
Published under exclusive licence by Emerald Publishing Limited
doi:10.1108/978-1-83608-064-020241002

emphasises the fact that in the socio-economic development process in a country, rural areas must not be ignored, and that the development process there must be made interesting so that the local people volunteer to actively participate in the process.

Rural marketing takes different forms even within a country simply because these markets are often different in structures and serve different kinds of customers.

This work is primarily based on the author's experience, which he gained while visiting many rural markets in developing countries.

This work has been developed over nine chapters:

Chapter 1: Certain Basic Concepts and the Background to Rural Marketing
Chapter 2: What is Development
Chapter 3: Hindrances to Rural Development
Chapter 4: Regulatory Measures Required for Rural Marketing and Sales
Chapter 5: Sources of Finance for Rural Marketing and Development
Chapter 6: Whether Socio-Economic Development may be Achieved Through
    Rural Marketing
Chapter 7: ICC International Code of Direct Selling, 2013
Chapter 8: ICC Advertising and Marketing Communications Code, 2018
Chapter 9: Development and the Issue of the Protection and Preservation of
    the Environment

In developing the theme of this work, primary sources of information have been relied upon, where possible. Secondary sources of information have also been referred to, where necessary.

It is sincerely hoped that this work will add a new practical dimension to the socio-economic development process in developing countries, in general.

Chapter 1

Certain Basic Concepts and the Background to Rural Marketing

Abstract

People, in general, seem to maintain a rather elementary meaning of rural marketing. Although there exists certain common features of rural marketing, there does not exist as yet, a reliable published work on this concept. The methods of rural marketing are very different from marketing in urban areas. These differences have usually occurred for a variety of reasons especially (a) paying careful attention to the development of urban markets and (b) a development in the marketing sector in the urban areas would be more visible than what they might be in the rural areas.

However, rural marketing stands for developing a form of marketing suitable for the rural areas. In this process of marketing, the marketeers and promoters will be required to consider the rural prejudices of the inhabitants therein, including those of the women consumers too. These markets also lack infrastructures, goods on demand are often different from those of the urban markets and lack of facilities proves to be a hazard for the suppliers of products. Nevertheless, it has been maintained in this work that rural marketing can be developed when it becomes a policy issues.

Keywords: Rural; urban; marketing; prejudices; infrastructure

1.1 Introduction

Although the concept of rural marketing has been with us for some time, not many direct major works seem to exist on the market. It is elementary that villages in the world outnumber cities and towns, and yet no consolidated policies or works have been developed on rural marketing; only opinions of certain authors exist.

The methods of rural marketing are different from those of marketing in urban areas, but nevertheless there exist certain common elements/factors in both types of marketing, namely, non-misrepresentation of goods and services, consumer

Rural Marketing as a Tool for National Development, 3–11

Copyright © 2024 Charles Chatterjee

Published under exclusive licence by Emerald Publishing Limited

doi:10.1108/978-1-83608-064-020241001

protection, health, safety standards, etc.; in order to clarify these concepts and practices, it is intended to define certain basic concepts relevant to rural marketing, in addition to the background to it.

1.2 Certain Basic Concepts Relevant to Rural Marketing

1.2.1 What Is Rural Marketing?

Rural marketing stands for a system of developing marketing concepts for rural areas and implementing them in practice through distribution and sales. It is a special kind of marketing, which is exclusively addressed to the rural population. The essentials of rural marketing may vary from one rural area to another around the world. The concept of rural marketing should be addressed to the rural population, i.e., a community of consumers and users of services who have not had the privilege of being introduced to products and services to which the urban population are easily introduced. Rural sales must be concerned with the products and services, which would be most suitable for the rural people under rural conditions and affordable to them. One of the principal aims of rural marketing and sales would be to create demands for goods and services affordable to them, and eventually allow the rural population to be engaged in the production process so that gradually and eventually those people take interest in them, and capacity is built in due course. The average income of the rural people will be the driving force to determine the level of demands for products and services. Rural marketing therefore is a system of marketing, which will entail an effective distribution network and cater for the requirements of the rural and urban population in accordance with the level of their economic demands.

1.2.2 Rural Distribution Networks

In most cases, the distribution network for introducing products and services to rural customers remains traditional, in consequence of which the supply of products and services primarily rely on distribution by wholesellers in urban areas to retailers in rural areas. The current distribution system is slow and expensive owing to interventions by middlemen. High transportation costs are also involved in this process. In a typical village in many parts of the world, the distribution network system remains primitive owing to the lack of communication systems, including the very primitive forms of rails, roads and even ports. Rural distribution network requires to be upgraded preferably with governmental intervention, after sufficient priority has been accorded to it. Furthermore, improvement of the communication system is a prerequisite for improving the rural marketing and sales systems. The usual channels of publicity through radio and television should be vigorously utilised in developing networks for rural marketing and sales. By the same token, it may be maintained that it is primarily through governmental participation that improvement and regular maintenance of rural infrastructure, particularly roads and transportation system may be ensured.

1.2.3 Rural Tradition – Prejudices

Rural tradition that is often based on their individual prejudices for or against certain products and/or services may initially be construed as a hindrance by marketeers. A thoughtful marketeer or a service provider should not make any attempt to criticise the rural people's consumption habit or even the traditional services they receive for household purposes; instead, they should politely try to introduce new products and services by explaining to them the comparative merits and disadvantages of using the traditional products over which certain urban firms or providers of services (including insurance policies, or savings of funds, etc.) have established their monopoly. The caution must be entered that marketing and sales in rural areas should be attempted with utmost politeness. Rural people are as intelligent as urban people, the principal distinguishing element between the rural and urban people would be that the former may lack the latest information on a product or a service.

Rural marketing and sales entail two important tasks:

(1) to break the barriers of the traditional consumer habits based on perhaps prejudices and
(2) to introduce new products and services in a polite but convincing manner without bearing any prejudice against rural customers.

No attempts should be made to hurt them by criticising their tradition – prejudices or consumption habits. A fine balance is thus required to be struck to protect the rural consumption habit, on the one hand, and yet to introduce new products and services on the other. In the final analysis, it must be the choice of consumers whether they would like to depart from their traditional consumption habit and opt for the new products. Some of the essential factors to tilt the balance towards the new products or services would be the price; the use of the products and/or services; the attractiveness of the product or services; the ease with which these may be used; and of course, the health and safety issues.

Ideally, it might be easier to introduce new products and services if they are manufactured or developed by indigenous means and by the indigenous people. Such a sentiment seems to be quite high in rural areas. It is reiterated that whilst tradition-based rural products must be allowed to stay on the markets, at the same time new products and services with their merits and disadvantages should be introduced to rural customers to see for which products and services they would eventually opt.

1.2.4 Rural Marketing and Rural Sales

In reality, there is no reason why the basic elements of marketing (Product, Price, Place and Promotion) may not apply to rural marketing too.[1] The theme of this work is that rural areas have been consistently ignored by the urban marketeers

---

[1]Some maintain that there are six Ps in marketing.

for a very long time perhaps in the unfounded belief that rural demands for products and services may not be as high as urban demands for products and services. It is possible to acquire a wide market for products and services in rural areas, economies of scale can become evident over a short period of time and the essentials of marketing may also be implemented in rural areas in any country.

It is to be emphasised that the principles of rural marketing may not be significantly different from those of urban marketing, although the demand structure should be initially determined by introducing new and smart products and services and by encouraging the rural people to be engaged in the manufacturing process of these products/goods.[2] Of course, the distribution network and the conditions of the basic infrastructure in rural areas will initially appear to be very different from those that usually exist in urban areas, but it is through rural marketing and sales and marketing of services to households that the distribution facilities and infrastructure may be improved.

One should appreciate that if rural marketing, sales of products and services are successful, then the total demand and sales of products and services in rural areas would far exceed than in urban areas. Rural marketing and sales therefore need a holistic approach from the government concerned in terms of policy-making, prioritisation coupled with a developed distribution network, which so far do not seem to have been prioritised in most cases.

1.3 Background to Rural Marketing

It would be inappropriate to discuss rural marketing and sales and rendering of services to rural areas without providing certain basic characteristics of rural areas generally. This should enable one to identify the issues that seem to be essential for developing and promoting rural marketing, sales and services in rural areas, in general, and suggest certain possible improvements that may be achieved generally by all developing countries.

The purpose is not to describe rural areas; instead, the characteristics of rural area-based demands, the consumers' aspirations and opportunities for marketing, sales and services have received attention. It is to be emphasised however that this discussion is based on certain general similarities in a broad sense that one may find in rural areas; concentration on particular rural areas has been avoided. It would be impractical and inadvisable too to identify the finer characteristics of rural areas in certain parts of the world in a work of this nature and size.

1.4 Some Basic Characteristics of Rural Areas

Rural areas in the developed world and those in the developing world are significantly different in that the former is usually well-served by the urban areas. Furthermore, rural areas in the developed world are often regarded as symptoms of wealth and luxury, which is not the case in the developing world. In view of

---

[2]This issue has received attention in Chapter 6 of this work.

these basic differences between the rural areas in the developed and developing worlds, rural marketing, sales and services do not usually get as much attention as those in the developed world. Rural markets in the developed world are in effect treated as extensions of urban markets. The providers of goods and services in most cases can serve the rural community extremely well.

Another important issue that should be pointed out is that the climate in most of the developed countries in the West are cold except those that border the Mediterranean. Nevertheless, these countries should pay attention to the effect of the looming climate change. Goods and services in a cold climate and those in a tropical climate are significantly different; thus, climatic conditions are an important factor in determining what types of goods and services should be provided; furthermore, the issues relating to their presentation, maintenance and life cycle prove to be an extremely important factor in developing marketing, sales and services in rural areas in the developing world.

Most of the rural areas in the developing world lack infrastructure, that is, they lack appropriate roads, distribution networks, communication systems as they also lack basic education particularly among women. These deficiencies have far-reaching effect on production, market-factoring and supply of goods and services. The lack of facilities of these basic factors operates as a deterrent to providers of goods and services in entering into rural areas and providing the goods and services as they do in the urban areas in the developing world.

In developing countries, in general, rural population usually are not very wealthy; thus, reasonably priced products and services are to be introduced to them, at least during the initial stages of marketing and sales. However, in a subsequent chapter of this work, it has been clearly suggested that rural products should be developed at a rural level, and that the indigenous people should be offered opportunities to learn the mechanics of service industries too. This process should also decrease the flow of migration from the rural areas to the urban areas in a country; in fact, it would be possible to have the migration flow reversed – from the urban areas to the rural areas in a country.

Multi-dimensional policies should be adopted and implemented by the government concerned whereby sectors such as education (skill-based) and health are prioritised, and the initial fund should be sought from various aid agencies rather than from any foreign government; the national government should also contribute to the development process as much as it can.

Through the initiatives of the national government and non-governmental bodies cost-effective and yet relevant programmes for rural development should be launched, which would make the rural people interested in participating in their own development goals. It is important to emphasise that the rural markets should be the 'feeders' at least initially for the urban areas in a country.

This work maintains that involvement of rural people in rural production and manufacturing process will offer them encouragement to improve on their own economy and other related issues, such as, education, health, etc., but governmental assistance will be needed. Rural marketing, sales and services should be regarded as a springboard for socio-economic development process in the rural areas of a country.

Issues of health and the environment are the two important factors that seem to plague most of the rural areas in the developing world. The causal connection between the conditions of life in rural areas and a high incidence of diseases are obvious. The lack of sanitation combined with the lack of education, nutrition and prejudices are but a few factors that have a negative effect on rural life. Rural people find agriculture as their basic source of employment and income, and not so surprisingly, most of the rural economies in most parts of the developing world are agriculture-based, and that is not sufficiently mechanised either.

Where agriculture is not an all-the-year-round activity, many rural people remain unemployed almost half of the year; incidentally, in India, for example, for over three decades now, agriculture has become an all-the-year-round activity; human resources for that period of time usually do not remain unutilised. This is the result of the programme of saving water during the rainy season and sprinkle them during the scorching summer season.

On the other hand, heavy rainfall often adversely affects the rural economies culminating in floods, which, in turn, leads to destruction of houses (mainly huts), unmetalled roads, and a variety of diseases take place. There is no reason why rural marketing, sales and services may not be addressed to the basic issues concerning the rural population. Gradually, providers should introduce materials for education, and a new style of marketing, sales and services whereby an everlasting changeover from agriculture to small-scale industries may be set up. These industries may eventually operate as a springboard for higher and sophisticated industries, which might bring in a change in the buying habits of the rural people.

Rural marketing, sales and services are a matter of policy. New ideas coupled with an understanding of how a large number of products may be introduced to rural areas should be seriously considered by the policy-makers. Additionally, policies and strategies as to how to break new grounds should receive the urgent attention of the policy-makers too. Giving rural people hope of a better life by the policy-makers at a rural level, should motivate them to take the initiative to do development work themselves.

1.5 Governmental Participation and Rural Marketing Sales and Services

Rural marketing, sales and services are the causes; rural development would be the effect. The developed world clearly exemplifies the fact that without governmental participation in a proactive role nothing much may be achieved by a country. Despite the fact that the private sector, which is primarily a profit-driven sector, often take part in the improvement of societal issues in the developed world, it falls on the public sector to take the initiative to liaise with non-governmental institutions as well as the private sector industries to determine policies and targets, and where possible, to involve the private sector and the rural initiatives too.

Given the nature of the problems that developing countries, in general, experience, one must appreciate that it is a very difficult task to change a country's economy over a short period of time particularly when historically the infrastructural development of these countries has never received much attention for a very long time.

Instead of living in history, this work would suggest that through cohesive plans and targets developed by governmental authorities, non-governmental institutions and private industries, where possible, attempts should be made to initiate development work in rural areas and the rationale for it has already been explained in the early part of this chapter. It is re-emphasised that governmental support would be essential for achieving socio-economic development in any country be it a rich or a poor country.

Rural development may be best achieved by involving the local people and the plan for development should be developed according to their aspirations. Democracy, at least in its popular sense, must be the form of government in all developing countries so that people therein are allowed to form their own 'action groups' which will have access to the relevant public departments in order to enable them to have consensual socio-economic development programmes.

The causal link between rural marketing, sales and services and a socio-economic development programme is important. There does exist a concomitant relationship between the two. What is most needed is an understanding on the part of everybody concerned in a socio-economic development process that large markets exist in rural areas. Development of markets in those areas will also open up opportunities for employment, which would lead to higher income, savings and investment.

1.6 Rural Consumers and Rural Marketing, Sales and Services

The success of rural marketing, sales and services depends very much on identification of the needs of rural consumers. In rural areas, the nature of demand for products and the types of products for which demands become evident is different from those that may be found in urban areas. In view of the special circumstances and conditions in rural areas, these consumers may not be able to do what is commonly known as 'bulk purchase' unless high demand exists for very essential products such as rice or staple food. Storage of consumer products presents problems in rural areas in view of the lack of preservation facilities, but this would not mean that the nature of demands may not be changed, and this is where the need for introducing new products to consumers becomes relevant. To put it simply, rural marketing, sales and services should be addressed to two important issues among others: (a) to cater for the basic needs and (b) to introduce affordable new products to diversify the needs and demands. It needs to be stressed that in rural marketing, sales and services, the introduction of new affordable products proves to be important.

In view of the absence of any standard income distribution structure in rural areas, pricing of products deserves special attention. Rural sales, in particular, should be based on maximum sales rather than sales to targeted and limited number of customers. A low pricing of products without compromising the quality may be achieved by setting up industries in the local areas and the lower costs of production will have advantage over pricing.

Rural sales can be seasonal too. Many rural areas are adversely affected by heavy rainfall; therefore, a tendency to store essential products becomes evident amongst rural consumers. It might be an idea to provide services whereby consumers may obtain their goods from direct delivery from suppliers, which has become a common practice in the Western world.

Two factors among others seem to be responsible for the lack of high demands for certain products in rural areas: (a) low income and (b) climatic conditions, which might not prompt majority of consumers to go out shopping. To this may be added another factor, which is, their lack of awareness of alternative products. Rural marketing and sales of products and services may flourish significantly if opportunities for sales and services are increased by setting up as many outlets as possible; this has another advantage in that consumers will not be deterred from buying products if the outlets are located within a reasonable distance. Currently, in most rural areas, good shopping centres are not available in the vicinity of residential areas. Setting up of shopping centres with facilities for light entertainment, which are very common in the Western world, can also be done by developing countries in their rural areas. The problems of rural marketing, sales and services are not solely concerned with finance, but with the techniques of promoting demands and introducing novel and affordable products to rural customers, and also making shopping enjoyable.

One of the means of increasing demands for products in rural areas would be to give publicity in the most effective and cost-effective ways, namely, through the local media, newspapers and even hand bills. There is no reason why introduction of sample products may not be included in the rural marketing and sales process.

Exposure to goods and creation of awareness are essential conditions of promoting rural marketing and sales. It might be an idea for schools to teach general business studies at the secondary level with a view to making young students aware of the essentials of Business Studies and Marketing, which might provide an impetus among the rural population to operate a sophisticated form of marketing in rural areas and they should also be informed of the techniques of and procedures for setting up and operating businesses in rural areas. Consumers are required to be made aware of alternative products, but all marketing, sales and services must be done in conformity with the ethics prevalent in the business.

Financial resourcefulness of consumers is another factor for increasing economic demand. In the developed world, economic demand is apparently a false concept in that the demand is buttressed by loan facilities (usually by credit cards). In reality, a rural area does not have similar level of demands, but the lack of finance often deters customers from buying products. This difficulty may be overcome by two means: (a) by maintaining an affordable price level and (b) by gradually providing credit facilities through the local rural banks. What is needed is to provide rural consumers opportunities in terms of ideas, finance and logistics for improving their distribution network.

1.7 Conclusions

It may be observed that the current unsophisticated style of rural marketing, sales and services is a product of the unhelpful perception maintained by the business community. It has been explained in this chapter that rural marketing, sales and services have remained almost untried. The materialistic attitude of consumers may not rationally be kept confined to urban people only. It is to be reiterated that in view of the bulk of the population living in rural areas in developing countries, there is no reason for maintaining that the total income from the rural population may not outweigh the incomes from the urban population in a country.

Chapter 2

What Is Development?

Abstract

There does not exist any precise definition of 'development'. In view of the indispensability of an interpretation of this concept a degree of speculation seems to exist in a development process. This is the reason this chapter has been included in this work. No scholar has precisely defined 'development' and 'developing' countries. It is believed that indigenous people know best what would be most suitable for them for development of their country. However, any discussion of these topics becomes incomplete, controversial, etc. in the absence of any precise definition. This chapter is no exception to this although an attempt has been made to outline development.

Keywords: Countries; developing; definition; development; interpretation

2.1 Introduction

Published works on development studies are in abundance in many markets in both the Western and the so-called developing countries too. The term 'so-called' has been used since there also does not exist any precise definitions of 'developed' and 'developing' countries. These classifications of countries were therefore based on the assumptions that the formerly colonised countries, particularly, in Africa, Asia, the Middle East, Latin America and the Caribbean should be called 'developing' countries, and the rest of the countries in the world would be known as 'developed' countries. The OECD's classification of countries is, by the same token, based on similar assumptions. Ironically, there are certain countries in the Western Europe, which may be considered to be poorer than China and India, to provide a limited number of examples.

If the academic studies on development were so effective, the question remains why then the de-colonised countries in the developing world, the majority of which are approximately 50 or so years old, still remain poor? Furthermore, 'economic development' should not be the most appropriate expression in this context, as without societal development, there may not be any proper development.

Rural Marketing as a Tool for National Development, 13–39
Copyright © 2024 Charles Chatterjee
Published under exclusive licence by Emerald Publishing Limited
doi:10.1108/978-1-83608-064-020241003

It is true that even now many of the regimes in the former colonies do have controversial political administrations in consequence of which people are denied their basic rights and freedoms, including their right to education whether by making the process expensive or by virtue of the lack of educational institutions or whatever; and, of course, often or in general, they are not allowed any critical voice against the political administrations, even though the latter is often self-centred or corrupt or effectively dictatorial. Thus, the general picture of the poor countries is rather dismal and worrying. An effective action for the development of these countries including their socio-economic development is urgently needed.

Only injections of money or other forms of aid may not add anything to anything. Rich countries are rich for a variety of reasons, namely, they are mindful of providing education in all possible disciplines to their citizens; they allow them to enjoy their basic rights and freedoms and are also allowed to voice their criticisms against governmental policies, whenever and wherever necessary. This provides their citizens a degree of confidence in them, allowing them to become sufficiently politically aware of the issues to which a country might need an urgent attention of their government.

The central theme of this work is that 'development' must come from within, that is, primarily through the efforts made by indigenous people as they should have more local knowledge than anybody else.[1] The Millennium Development Goals (MDGs), which outlined how development should be achieved over a 15-year period, came to an end in 2015, and the Goals have been replaced by Sustainable Development Goals (SDGs), which plans to achieve its targets by 2030. This process of development has recently been interjected by, for example, cross-border migrations, population displacement leading to a global refugee crisis. The issue of security has also gained extreme importance in development studies like the protection and preservation of the environment, climate change and the relevant public awareness worldwide.

According to Rist, the origins of Western philosophy of development may be found in the works of St Augustine and Aristotle.[2] On the other hand, views exist to confirm that the concept of development could be found in some of the European thinkers such as Auguste Comte, which was triggered by the socio-economic upheavals occasioned by industrialisation.[3]

Whatever might be the old history of development it may safely be maintained that with the commencement of the de-colonisation process after the Second World War, the issue of socio-economic development became a burning issue, particularly for the de-colonised countries. However, developed countries do also

---

[1]See further S K Chatterjee, 'International Law of Development', *Encyclopaedia of Public International Law* (1986), Max Planck Institute for Comparative Public Law and International Law.

[2]G Rist, *History of Development: From Western Origins to Global Faith*, 2nd edition, London, Zed Books (2002).

[3]See further M P Cowen and R W Shenton, *Doctrines of Development*, London, Routledge (1996).

go through a continuing process of socio-economic development, but strangely enough, the term 'development' is, in general, associated with the former colonies that started gaining independence after the end of the Second World War. Incidentally, as stated earlier, there does not exist any precise definition of a 'developed' or a 'developing' country.[4] Many seem to believe that 'developing' countries predominantly stand for the former colonies. Thus, scholars and authors have been examining and writing on 'development', a concept, the characteristics of which remain undefined. It ought to be mentioned that many of the so-called developing countries have very rich 'cultural' histories too, although that may not match the current cultural level achieved by many of the developed States. Despite a definitional vacuum existing, everybody tends to proceed with the idea that all poor countries share similar socio-economic symptoms without identifying their strengths in regard to dormant human resources and the potential capacity of these countries in re-cycling the proceeds of their national resources with scientific and technical help of the developed States. Rather than leaving it to be a matter of domestic jurisdiction, most of the developing countries, if not all, are victims of dictatorial administration based on prejudices, and the ancient ideas of hierarchical governmental structures. In other words, public and private (corporate entities) administration systems should be participatory.

Rather than allowing them financial aid, they need knowledge, both technical and otherwise, and they themselves should be involved in the development process in their countries. In order to satisfy the readers, certain basic information should also be provided, and an attempt to that end has been made in the following section of this chapter.

2.2 A Brief Account of the Progression of the Concept of Development

In this section an attempt has been made to briefly examine the progression of the concept of 'development' over the decades.

2.2.1 The Period Between 1940 and 1950

United Nations was set up in 1945, to achieve development of the basic rights and duties particularly of the de-colonised countries, for international co-operation in order to maintain peace and security in the world. At the same time, it placed emphasis on the issue of socio-economic development too. In order to achieve the latter, various institutions were set up, such as the Economic and Social Council (ECOSOC), the World Bank initially, which eventually became the World Bank Group, and the International Monetary Fund (IMF) among others. In fact, the actual title of the World Bank is significant – the International Bank for Re-Construction (post–Second World War reconstruction) and Development (IBRD), which gradually became the World Bank Group, although some of the

---

[4]See further S K Chatterjee, 'International Law of Development', op. cit.

components of this Group were set-up even in the 1960s and in the 1970s, such as the International Development Association (IDA), Multi-lateral Investment Guarantee Agency (MIGA), the International Centre for Settlement of Investment Disputes (ICSID) and the IBRD Panel of Experts, the latter, for dealing with the complaints, if any, from the beneficiary States. Each of these institutions has provided platforms for development-related issues and activities.

Incidentally, prior to the UN decades, that is, during the League of Nations period, the concept of Development was almost absent, some of the development policies had been advanced during the 1920s and 1930s; the League was very much concerned with issues of warfares and arrived at what may be described as humanising warfares whatever the expression might have meant from a legal standpoint. The only reference to socio-economic issues could be found in Article 23(e) of the League Covenant, which provided that[5]:

> ... will make provision to secure and maintain freedom of communications and of transit and equitable treatment for the commerce of all Members of the League. In this connection, the special necessities of the regions devastated during the war of 1914–1918 shall be borne in mind.

The concept of 'development' became prominent as from the days of de-colonisation, but it should be borne in mind that most of the 'developers' were not familiar with the techniques and processes involved in a socio-economic development process. Furthermore, there had occurred what may be described as a 'pull back' factor in the development process. In general, the colonised peoples' aspirations were to become equal to the colonial powers, which, in reality, were fraught with difficulties. The lack of intellectual reservoirs in the former colonies presented an insurmountable hindrance to the development process. The former colonised people, in general, wanted to copy the Western world in their country, without realising that the infrastructures and intellectual reservoir were not imitable in those countries, and for whatever reasons, the governments of the newly-born States, in general, failed to encourage people by providing facilities to become creative in intellectual ideas.

The concept of 'development' is not an entirely new one; it could be traced as far back as the 1920s and 1930s. Great Britain and France, the two most powerful colonial powers, thought of 'development' of their colonies too. Indeed, in 1929, the Colonial Development Act was passed by the government of Great Britain to provide aid to the British colonies. This was followed suit by the French government. In 1946, the *Fonds d'Investissements pour le Developpement Économique et Social* (FIDES) was set up for similar purposes applicable to the former French colonies. It was stated in this work that aid may be necessary in certain urgent cases, but it may not contribute to any development process. But after the Second World War was over, the US President Truman, delivered his address outlining

---

[5]See *International Law Documents*, 13th edition, Oxford University Press (2017), at 7.

his ideas about development in then popular term 'underdeveloped countries'.[6] In his address he emphasised, inter alia, that the former colonies should look to the United States as a model to emulate. He wanted the world to embark upon a bold programme whereby the underdeveloped countries would benefit from the scientific and industrial progress achieved by the United States. He announced his plan for a 'fair deal' for the rest of the world.[7]

The initial period of de-colonisation was marked by euphoria of the former colonised people, without knowing how to handle their independence and what would be the procedures for socio-economic development in those jurisdictions. They turned to the former colonial powers to undertake this job; but, in reality, they failed to realise that only industrialisation of the economies and some basic learning at schools and universities would not suffice; actual human resource development would be essential, which in most cases were not achieved. Only exploitation of natural resources in those countries became the primary source of income for both the newly-born countries and the foreign corporations. The rural areas were neglected.

During the period of de-colonisation, the new administrations were not clear about the agenda they should have adopted for their country's benefits; consequently, the levels of economic and financial dependence of the former colonies on their respective colonial powers became high and, in many cases, came to a point of no-return. It is to be emphasised in this context that political independence without economic independence is meaningless; and this is precisely what happened to the non-white British and French colonies for example, particularly during the first decade of their development process.

Truman's Declaration also received criticisms primarily on the grounds that it was a deal 'in veil' so to say to establish another form of colonisation by the United States of the developing areas; incidentally, by the time Truman delivered his speech on a New Deal, certain former colonies already declared their political independence. Truman's declaration ran counter to the opinions held by some of the nationalist leaders in some of the former British colonies, namely Gandhi, Nkrumah and Nyerere, as they maintained that development would be part of their efforts to achieve independence. But, unfortunately, over the years, particularly during the 1950s and 1960s, a new kind of concept of development emerged, which on reflection, may be described as a product of confusion among the minds of leaders, which effectively defeated the primary objectives of socio-economic development of the former colonies. This has been examined in the subsequent passages of this work.

---

[6]See further U Kothari, 'From Colonial Administration to Development Studies: A Postcolonial Critique of the History of Development Studies 1', U Kothari (ed) *A Radical History of Development Studies*, London, Zed Books (2005), at 47–66.

[7]H S Truman, 'Inaugural Address', (1949), *Documents on American Foreign Relations*, Princeton, Princeton University Press (1967).

2.2.2 The Period Between 1960 and 1970

For development purposes, this period was characterised by UN resolutions and guidelines, including those adopted by some of its offices. There is no need to examine each of those resolutions, recommendations, declarations; it would be sufficient to itemise the most relevant ones for the reader:

- Declaration on the Granting of Independence to Colonial Countries and Peoples, 1960,
- The General Assembly Resolution on Permanent Sovereignty over Natural Resources, 1962,
- It was during the 1960s that the UN Development Decade also started.

After achieving self-determination (de-colonisation), many of the former colonies acted in accordance with paragraph four of the 1962 UN General Assembly Resolution entitled Permanent Sovereignty over Natural Resources, and in most cases, the compensation for nationalising the assets of the foreign entities was paid for. Nevertheless, these acts performed by the newly-born countries became a source of dissatisfaction for developed countries. However, history suggests that developed countries also went through a similar process long before the de-colonisation process started.[8]

The de-colonisation process has produced, amongst others, an adverse effect on each of the former colonies; almost each of them wanted to copy the characteristics of their respective colonial powers, without appreciating that their societal structure and industrial capacity would not allow them to achieve their unachievable targets. Owing to the lack of preparation for establishing the appropriate kind of governments to suit their circumstances, the majority of the newly-born countries followed the pattern of governments, which acted as their former colonial powers. Education did not become universal; hardly any effective provision for building human resources was created, other than for a few well-known universities such as the four chartered universities in India and a few reputable universities in certain chosen jurisdictions. Most of the former colonies relied on the revenues that they received from their natural resources, and their debt-burden became too high; the proceeds of sale of natural resources was not high enough to cater for the compulsory expenditures required for the running of the country. Furthermore, the International Monetary Fund (IMF) and the International Development Association (IDA) and their lending agencies may not have agreed to provide loans, unless the economy of the country concerned maintained a favourable balance of payments position. The newly-born countries are therefore long overdue to achieve economic self-sufficiency by and through private foreign investors in their country preferably on negotiated terms, and by adopting and implementing effective socio-economic programmes for self-development.

---

[8]See further B Katzarov, *The Theory of Nationalisation*, Springer (1964).

Development of countries may not be achieved by applying any uniform formula – one size does not fit all. Every country's history, geography, societal attitudes, availability of human resources and natural resources, geographical and political conditions among others should be considered; otherwise, even the objectives of capacity-building may not be attained. Then, as stated earlier, the socio-economic development in the rural areas in a country forms the backbone to that country's socio-economic development as a whole.

Furthermore, freedoms and rights of peoples in a country must be guaranteed, and these will not only give confidence in the minds of the people but also a recognition of their identity. They must also be required to perform their duties towards their people and the country. The question remains however whether any of these may be achieved by a country when her regime is dictatorial rather than democratic. The validity of this statement may be confirmed by reflecting on the nature of administrations in the majority of the countries in the West until the end of the Second World War. Interestingly enough, none of the dictatorial countries in the world has proved to be a developed country with rights and freedoms allowed to her people. Access to an impartial justice system is another very important symptom of a democratic country. However, the judiciary of a country should be separable and separate from the executive as it is in England. But this is not possible to achieve by any country that is subject to a dictatorial form of government. In this connection, one may like to peruse and follow the guidelines offered by the United Nations through the Charter of Economic Rights and Duties of States, 1972.[9] Although they represent guidelines especially for diplomatic/commercial negotiators, it is worth following this document to acquire a new dimension to development, at least how it should be achieved, and for achieving development, freedoms and rights of peoples in a society must be safeguarded.

Development seems to have lost its ethics; it is now often regarded as a business; its objectives are not only economic development but also societal. As stated earlier, the maintenance of it and its continuing growth process should not be hindered, and in order to ensure its continuing growth process, capacity building of the indigenous people proves to be essential. This is the relationship between development and capacity-building. The primary functions of developers are twofold: (a) to create the foundation for 'containable' development, that is, the level of development a country's indigenous people can nurture and (b) in order to achieve the latter, it is for the developers to build capacity of the indigenous people so that they themselves may contribute to their country's development process.

However, 'development' seems to have a negative aspect too. A developed economy can be a point of jealousy for people of another developing country. In view of the absence of any progressive development process in many developing

---

[9]UN Publication Sales No. E73.II. D.4, Annex 1.A; see also S K Chatterjee, 'The Charter of Economic Rights and Duties of States: An Evaluation after Fifteen Years', *International and Comparative Law Quarterly* (1991).

countries primarily owing to the lack of any effective development policy adopted and operated by the public authorities in those countries, the tendency to emigrate into the developed world rises; thus, the public authorities in developing countries should adopt a continuing development process, which should primarily be achieved by and through the indigenous people, and the reasons thereof, have already been explained in this chapter.

Development should be country-specific and people-specific. Thus, imitation of a development process may not be helpful. Policy-makers in developing countries should also adopt and implement country-specific and people-specific development.

2.3 Development and Progress

Development leads to progress, provided it builds capacity, including intellectual capacity. However, the caution should be entered that not everyone may be as intellectually advanced; but capacity-building is a multi-dimensional activity in that it offers every participant an opportunity to assess his/her ability in a particular dimension to a capacity-building process.

The Declaration on the Granting of Independence to Colonial Countries and Peoples combined with the UN General Assembly Resolution entitled Permanent Sovereignty over Natural Resources seem to have given the newly-born countries a new impetus to take the initiative to be engaged in the development process in their country. A new kind of awareness seems to have developed in the minds of developing countries leading to the adoption of a rather new type of resolutions through the initiative of the UN General Assembly. The following are the examples of some such resolutions:

- The New International Economic Order (NIEO) and
- The Charter of Economic Rights and Duties of States, 1972.

The 1970s also witnessed a growing awareness of the peoples in the developing world of the need for the protection and preservation of the environment. In 1972, the *Stockholm Conference (UN) on the Human Environment* was held. Then, of course, came the *Rio Declaration* of 1992.[10,11] However, despite adopting a number of reasonably good resolutions, declarations or conventions, one should reflect on the progress achieved by these instruments particularly in the rural areas of a country, which, as stated earlier, form the backbone to a country.

Financial policies addressed to the peoples in rural areas in developing countries should be adopted, the consequences of which are clear. International organisations formulate principles, policies and guidelines in the hope that the Member States of the United Nations will implement them as much as they can. Regrettably, many of them have failed to adopt those guidelines and policies to

---

[10]https://www.un.org/en/conferences/environment/stockholm1972.
[11]See *International Law Documents*, 13th edition, Oxford University Press (2017), at 397.

rural areas, which would have enriched not only those areas but also the people within them. Rural areas should be the hinterland for the corresponding urban areas in a country.

Rather than relying upon foreign or international institutional aid, governments should allocate a reasonable fund to rural development and encourage indigenous charitable institutions to participate as donors but not as policy-makers. Rural people, as stated earlier, must have project-related education and training in all sectors of their economy, and eventually, become providers of materials for high industries, which usually operates in urban areas or nearby towns. This practice should gradually and eventually minimise the debts of their country, and the latter should become relatively economically self-sufficient. Of course, in order to achieve this, policy-makers should merely be observers, and advise the leaders in rural areas whether they are conforming to their policies or not. If external financial dependence grows in a development process, then the country's debt-burden will rise. Thus, where possible, as suggested above, both foreign companies and local financiers should be encouraged to contribute to finance and the foreign countries under contracts would be obliged to buy those products. It cannot be emphasised anymore that development must be achieved by local means and by the indigenous people with very little involvement of foreign trainers, and where necessary, only for capacity-building. Training centres for capacity-building should also be operated.

Local peoples' awareness of the need for the protection and preservation of the environment should be raised in their own interest. On this issue, leaders may like to work in collaboration with the local media (both radio and television) in order to ensure that the rural peoples' awareness on the issues of the environmental and climate change is raised. In fact, this should be part of the school curricula.

2.4 Difficulties in Defining International Development

There does not exist any universally agreed definition of the term 'development', but it is usually associated with the idea of material progress, which would entail eradication of poverty and minimise inequality between the rich and the poor. The intense desire of the poor, often endowed with intellectual and creative thoughts, remain unknown and are deprived of opportunities to become part of the mainstream society to lead a successful life – a loss of human resources. Socio-economic development for economic progress in a country must be combined with human resources development. But, unfortunately, the oppressive regimes in many parts of the world persistently disregarded this issue and the poor and the minorities have remained marginalised. It may be inferred that the lack of freedom for the people and, in particular, the poor and the minorities, are directly responsible for the lack of development in the sense of socio-economic progress in many of the developing countries.

It has already been emphasised that the issues of development are not universally applicable; each country and her people are different, as her needs. One of the important factors of socio-economic development is the development of human resources. Socio-economic development may not be measured by any mathematical or statistical means; it is an issue which should aim at a knowledge-based economy and society in order to form the platform for continuing the future growth. A knowledge-based economy should, over a short period of time, become innovative and inventive.

In her work entitled *International Development*, Anna Lanoszka, rightly pointed out the limitations of measuring economic progress in a country by referring to GDP (Gross Domestic Product). GDP is measured by referring to aggregate domestic spending, which includes 'consumer, business and government spending, investment spending and the country's net exports'.[12] One should not disregard the fact that most of the governments in the world, rich or poor alike, have high level of public debt. In this context, one may like to refer to Niall Ferguson's work entitled *The Great Degeneration* in which he pointed out, inter alia, the high level of public debt in the United States too. Any high level of public debt is a certain indicator of the weakness of an economy.[13] On the other hand, in determining a country's assets, the United Nations takes into account a country's (a) manufactured capital (for example, roads and technology); (b) human capital (for example, knowledge and health); and (c) natural capital (for example, natural resources and the atmosphere). Neither of the items at (a) may be developed by a country unless human capital has been developed. This is one of the basic themes of this work too.

Any theoretical and general perception of 'development' to be applied to all countries will not do; as stated earlier, that it has to be country-specific and human resources and natural resources specific. This should help form ideas about technology development. Technology, where possible, should be indigenous in nature; foreign technology increases dependence on them, an expensive game. This is the reason why this work has suggested that private foreign investors (transnational corporations) before entering into a developing country should be told to provide capacity-building to rural people, in particular, in that country, and that it should be part of their contractual obligations. It is for the State or central government concerned to remunerate the foreign investment company and the additional amount needed for remunerating the latter may be off-set by adopting buy-back or countertrade system.[14]

---

[12]A Lanoszka, *International Development: Socio-economic Theories, Legacies and Strategies*; London, Routledge (2018), at 4.

[13]N Ferguson, *The Great Degeneration – How Institutions Decay and Economies Die*, New York, Penguin Group (2013).

[14]The buy-back system is quite simple; it requires the foreign company to buy back the high-quality products that will be manufactured by the indigenous people upon completion of their training (capacity-building) and the foreign company can sell those products, which are cheaper than those manufactured in their home markets, at a high price both in their home markets and export markets. This way both parties will benefit, and their capacity-building fee may be off-set by the purchase price of the host country's products. See further C Chatterjee, *Legal Aspects of Trade Finance*, London, Routledge (2006), at 11.

In order to achieve development, policy-makers must decide this issue on a democratic basis, what may really be needed for their country and reliance upon foreign or institutional aid (International Development Association (IDA)), for example, should be minimised, if not totally eliminated. There is no reason why trained indigenous people may not be in course of time become innovative and inventive to meet their technological needs, and other needs, such as medicines and industrial products to name but a few. Alternatively, the government concerned, without taking any monetary aid, may ask for technological help. This is an affirmative meaning of aid which may be found in any standard dictionary.

It is submitted that the exploration and exploitation of sea resources, for example, would entail the engagement of foreign corporate entities many of which have the required technologies and expertise. But governments should realise that the demand for fine oil, for example, will gradually diminish by virtue of electrically-driven cars in most parts of the developed world; the demand for crude oil may therefore be mainly for industrial purposes. However, the demand for the latter product may also diminish if the rich countries find certain alternatives.

Incidentally, the vast majority of the developing countries are tropical countries; therefore, they should have projects for developing solar energy to meet their demands for clean energy and it is also extremely necessary for them to acquire training in order to ensure that they themselves may be engaged in developing this kind of energy and actually utilise it.

The social dimensions to development should not be undermined. In his work entitled *Development as Freedom* (A Sen, a Nobel Laureate), Sen emphasised the correlation between individual freedom and development.[15] This work has also emphasised that 'development' should be the outcome of peoples' participation in it, as they know their geographic areas best. However, governments must also play their role as fair rule-making bodies. This can best happen in a Federal State, such as India. Her constitution contains three lists of activities allocated to the central government and the component States – Union list, Concurrent list and the State list. Unless a country is a single State country, such as Singapore, development issues should be controlled by each State through participatory means rather than by directing the people through a hierarchical form of government. Peoples' freedom in doing things by themselves and for themselves should be the policy on which conditions of development should be based. This would stand for a learning process for them (as an aspect of capacity-building). There may not be any general theory of development – matters of development are localised; therefore, developmental policies should be based on local resources, including human and natural resources. Guidance as to development may be sought from foreign experts; but development work must be conceptualised by the local people and performed by them. It may not be based on others' examples, where similar examples do not exist. Governments must also provide the basic facilities, namely, banks catering particularly for the rural areas

---

[15]See further A Sen, *Development as Freedom*, New York, Random House (1999), at xii.

in a country, insurance companies, employment legislation (for protecting the rights of employees), legislation regarding protection of customer rights, and a participatory management system. At this point, it would be appropriate to refer to the opinions of some of the renowned economists; although they were not known as development economists, certain of their views are still relevant to modern day development debates.

2.4.1 Adam Smith (1723 – 1790)

There is hardly any economist who failed to refer to Adam Smith's work, where relevant. An 18th century Scottish social philosopher is considered to be the founding father of economic liberalisation. Perhaps, the contemporary society around him contributed to his developing the idea of economic liberalisation. Those were the days of rich and powerful landlords, who wanted to appease the peasants, and the powerful countries had an ambition to dominate the weaker countries – an indication of colonisations. Foreign imports of products were disliked by the then society lest they adversely affected the local production process. Accumulation of wealth in the form of ownership of land areas, metals including gold and silver, were highly regarded as elements of national wealth. Economic liberalisation was totally denied. Adam Smith despised the absence of economic liberalism, mercantilism, which abhorred innovation, and the lack of exploitation of human potential. Ironically, during the days of the industrial revolution all these were reversed.

In his work entitled *Inquiry into the Nature and Causes of the Wealth of Nations (1776)*, Smith advocated as minimum intervention as possible from the government. He was an ardent supporter of 'free market', although he at the same time maintained that governmental intervention would be necessary for maintaining law and order, collection of revenue particularly for the purposes of the defence of the country. Smith advocated human resources development including development of skills, specialisation in industries and incentives for new inventions. Some of these issues/items do come under the domain of a government, but basically, he advocated the *Laissez-faire* doctrine. Smith was against monopoly; but unfortunately, markets in most of the capitalist economies do now seem to believe in having large corporate entities with total monopoly over certain businesses; acquisitions and mergers have become a common phenomenon, and the small industries seem to suffer – a market feature that runs counter to the *Laissez-faire* doctrine; on the other hand, in a socialist economy, corporate entities, in general, are under government control. Both situations are contrary to Smith's economic philosophy.

2.4.2 John Maynard Keynes (1883 – 1946)

A British economist and diplomat who criticised many of the principles of classical economics. The industrial revolution that occurred in Great Britain seems to have influenced Keynes to promote the idea that economics should be a policy-oriented discipline, which would be more relevant to the changing world, significantly contributed to the industrial world. Governments' role in a policy-oriented discipline may not be denied. Keynes' very good work entitled *The Economic Consequences of Peace* was based on his protest over the Treaty of Versailles, 1919, and which, in effect, made him resign from the public office. The cause of his protest was mainly the unfairness towards Germany particularly with regard to reparation demands.[16] In fact, Keynes was proved right in that there exists a belief that the Treaty of Versailles was perhaps the main cause of the rise of Nazism, which paved the path of the Second World War. However, during the early 20s, Keynes rightly found the correlation between economy and peace, which the majority of the modern political leaders seem to fail to appreciate.

But his work which formed the basis for the importance of microeconomics and for which he is still remembered was entitled *The General Theory of Employment, Interest and Money*, in which he placed emphasis on the adverse effect of unemployment, inflation, low savings, high price level, etc. to make the governments aware of the contemporary state of the economic health of a country; in fact, it was Keynes who created the concept of GDP, which is now almost universally recognised.[17] Keynes also advocated fiscal and monetary policies in order to enable governments avoid recessions and economic booms.

Keynes was a supporter of governmental intervention in operating economic policies of countries rather than leaving it to the business community; to that extent, he advocated a limited play of the *Laissez-faire* doctrine.

In the current time, it must be appreciated that economic volatility often takes place owing to other economic behaviours; thus, it is mainly by and through interventions of governments that the effect of such volatilities of economies may be constructively dealt with. Furthermore, from a socio-economic point of view, it is the government's duty and responsibility to look after the economic interests of its own people. Keynes also supported the idea of full employment by governments rather than waiting for securing it by other means.

2.4.3 Frederick A von Hayek (1899 – 1992)

In order to understand Hayek's economic philosophy, one is required to appreciate that Hayek's participation in the First World War very much shaped his views on what bases economic policy of a country should be formed. He was totally dismayed by the inflationary spiral which occurred in Austria during the 1920s, and realised that a total governmental control of an economy may not be the most appropriate way of running the economy of a country. Hayek came to the conclusion that a total governmental direction would lead to an authoritarian command economy which would be another version of a socialist economy.

[16]J M Keynes, *The Economic Consequences of Peace*, New York, Harcourt, Brace and Howe (1920).
[17]J M Keynes, *The General Theory of Employment, Interest and Money*, Palgrave Macmillan (1936).

Indeed, in his work entitled *The Road to Serfdom*, Hayek expressed his support for free markets; however, although he in fact supported the *Laissez-faire* doctrine, he also to a certain extent supported governmental intervention in policy-making.[18]

Although the concept of *Laissez-faire* sounds extremely attractive, one is required to accept that the peoples' economy may not be regulated in an effective way, and the consequence of it would lead to socio-economic chaos. Hence in a country such as the United Kingdom, free market economy largely exists, but it is also highly regulated by the central bank (the Bank of England) and other commercial organisations, such as the British Bankers' Association or the Confederation of British Industries (CBI) or the Institute of Directors (IOD).

So, what is the relevance of all these theories advocated by Adam Smith, John Maynard Keynes or Van Hayek to the issue of development?

The governments of the vast majority of developing countries may like to consider the *Laissez-faire* doctrine to function in order to involve the people to the operation of this doctrine. It has already been emphasised in this work that socio-economic development must be achieved through the participation of the indigenous people, as it proves to be a learning process for them too.

At this point it would be interesting to reflect on some of the other opinions of eminent institutions and authors on the concept of 'development'. It should be pointed out however that the concept of 'development' prior to the de-colonisation period and during the de-colonisation period too were different. During the early years of Western development process, that is, after the Industrial Revolution took place in Great Britain, development stood for economic growth and industrialisation, an idea which seems to have attracted the attention of a good majority of the newly de-colonised countries. Perhaps, this is one of the reasons why the newly-born countries, in general, failed to achieve the development that they really needed; a quick industrialisation process without creating the foundations for growth and progress will not do.

It should be reiterated that before the de-colonisation commenced, the economy in Great Britain was dominated by two main concepts: one promoted by Adam Smith and the other by John Maynard Keynes. One followed economic liberalism, and the other effectively advocated governmental intervention particularly in relation to governmental affairs in order to make the markets subject to regulations. These two views created almost an indelible mark on the minds of many countries, including the newly-born ones.

The most indispensable work on the theory of development entitled *Theory of Economic Development* was by Joseph Schumpeter.[19] Schumpeter's support for economic liberalism seems to have prompted him to write this work. The other reason which also might have prompted Schumpeter to write his book on development was that according to him, many economists were detached from the

---

[18]F A Hayek, *The Road to Serfdom: Text and Documents*, Bruce Caldwell (ed) (1944), Illinois, University of Chicago Press (2007).
[19]J Schumpeter, *Theory of Economic Development*, Transaction Publishers (1981).

reality; thus, their works were merely theoretical studies. In his work, he emphasised a creative role of the entrepreneur who would encourage free market competition, innovations and inventions. Schumpeter's work did address the issue of development of the newly-born countries. His work is relevant to the de-colonised countries in that in order to develop their economies, they need strong entrepreneurs, inventive and innovative ideas, for which development of human resources would also be necessary.

Before entering into the problems of 'development' in the developing countries, it would be apposite to emphasise that prior to the beginning of the de-colonisation period, the concept of 'development' in the developed world, in general, was confined to two sub-concepts: (a) free market and (b) innovations and inventions – the latter need intellectual might. Perhaps, the Industrial Revolution which occurred in Great Britain largely influenced the minds of contemporary entrepreneurs. In fact, both these elements are very essential for the development of developing countries too. But, it is so important to remind the reader of the fact that irrespective of whether a former colony was under the control of Belgium, France, the Netherlands, Spain or Great Britain or any other colonial power, the common attribute of these powers was to impose on their colonies their own plans on any issue, whether education or judiciary, or any other discipline, but in their attempts to achieve socio-economic development, the developers, in general, seem to have failed to appreciate that each developing country and often their component States too are different from the others. Thus, often different plans of socio-economic development for each State would be necessary. This is what should be done by indigenous people, perhaps with the help of foreign corporate entities for a suitably short period of time.

Joseph Schumpeter's work – *Theory of Economic Development* – came out at a time when de-colonisation process had not started. He died in 1950, and the first country to be de-colonised was Indonesia (the Netherlands being their colonial power). But his idea of liberal economies and inventions and innovations are still relevant to achieving socio-economic development in developing countries. He advocated the progressive development of democratic institutions, which would eventually contribute to developing social cohesion.

2.4.4 Sir W Arthur Lewis (1915–1991)

The first pioneering researcher on 'development' with reference to the de-colonised countries was Sir W Arthur Lewis of St Lucia, a Caribbean Island. He studied at the London School of Economics, obtained his doctoral degree and became a professor first at the University of Manchester (UK) and then at Princeton University, US, where he worked for over 20 years. In 1955, Sir Arthur Lewis wrote his monumental work entitled *The Theory of Economic Growth*.[20] It should be appreciated that Lewis was a person who had a direct experience in a

---

[20]See W Arthur Lewis, *The Theory of Economic Growth*, Homewood, Illinois, Richard Irwin Inc (1955); see also Robert L Tignor, *W Arthur Lewis and the Birth of Development Economics*, Princeton, New Jersey, Princeton University Press (2005).

colonised country, St Lucia, a former British colony until she attained her independence in 1979.

Lewis rightly pointed out that the vast majority of the newly born States, if not all of them, had a dual economy: urban and rural. Whereas the urban areas aspired industrialisation, the rural areas, which were basically 'agricultural' in nature, were neglected by their government. Lewis firmly believed that instead of ignoring the agricultural sector in a country, it should be developed for quality products suitable for exports. In other words, rural areas needed to be developed as soon as possible; indeed, these areas had been neglected by the colonial powers too. Furthermore, he advocated that governments should stimulate inventions and innovations for strengthening the manufacturing sector too.

Lewis also maintained that the countries that have a large agricultural sector should develop that sector first, in order to ensure that its products are exportable. This is what Great |Britain also did and still does, although over the past years, the country has switched over to industrial products for exports, and raised the income of the country. By coincidence, the vast majority of the de-colonised countries have good agricultural sectors, which not only include farm products but also animal husbandry, irrigation etc. With very little training (capacity building), they should be able to achieve self-sufficiency, for example, India, a major food exporting country after meeting her own internal demand, has been doing such.

Lewis was also an ardent supporter of the development of human capital as a factor of 'development', which is often ignored by the majority of the developing countries.

Social pluralism is a very common phenomenon within the developing world. Thus, multi-party democracy rather than dictatorial governments would be the most suitable form of government as it would be participatory; consequentially, the indigenous people would take more interest in their country's development programmes. Lewis not only advocated improvement of human capital but also promoted the idea that workers must have access to education and healthcare.[21] One can thus maintain that Lewis' idea of socio-economic development of a country represented a comprehensive concept. Sir Arthur Lewis was awarded a Nobel prize in 1979 for his contribution to Economics.

2.4.5 Walt W Rostow (1916 – 2003)

Rostow's work entitled *The Stages of Economic Growth* is generally known as the work that supported modernisation through stages, for example, from an unstable or underdeveloped economy to a gradual transition by mainly promoting it to a

---

[21]See further R Lewis, 'Grenada: A Testing Ground for Lewis' Balanced Development Perspectives', *Journal of Social and Economic Studies*, Vol. 54, No. 4, at 206; see also M Yoichi, 'The Political Element in the Works of W Arthur Lewis: The 1954 Model and African Development', *Developing Economics*, Vol. XLIV, No. 3, at 339–340 (2006); see also by the same author also on the same title, op. cit., at 344–345.

take-off stage which should take place owing to technological advancement – a platform for further economic development, and gradually that economy should reach the stage of mass consumption which is a typical symptom of a rich market.[22]

From a theoretical perspective, Rostow's theory of progression of economies and modernisation may appear to be good; but it may not be a universally applicable theory as the conditions in developing countries, in general, are very different from those of the majority of the developed economies.

It has already been emphasised in this work that the vast majority of the developing countries consist of large rural areas, and that most of the governments of these countries mainly paid their attention to their urban areas. Rural areas often operate at the hinterlands for the urban areas in a country. One may like to exemplify the United Kingdom on this point.

The primary theme of this work has thus been precisely on the issue of how rural areas in a country may be developed bearing in mind that these areas, in general, lack basic infrastructure, education and health improvement facilities – hence capacity building is needed most.

After the de-colonisation period started, the UN appreciated the need for publishing a work on development. In the 1970s, the Commission on International Development published its Report, popularly known as the *Pearson Report* which Report was also known as *Partners in Development*.[23] This Report identified 30 major goals and its recommendations were categorised into 10 major categories including economic relief, aid, aid administration, technical assistance, population control, education, research and multilateral aid.

Apparently, Rostow's 'modernisation' theory which entailed different stages of economic growth influenced the setting up of development agencies, including aid agencies, based on the idea that funds and aid would augment the development process; indeed, this idea was widely accepted in the 1960s. During the Kennedy administration in the United States, the Foreign Assistance Act, 1961 was passed, and the US Agency for International Development (USAID) was created.

Interestingly enough, on the other side, even before the United Nations was established on 24 October 1945, the World Bank (IBRD) and the International Monetary Fund (IMF) were established for similar activities – loans, aid and pure lending to governments, in particular, to the governments of developing countries. In 1964, the UN Conference on Trade and Development (UNCTAD) was set up. The title of the organisation is self-explanatory and significant. The majority of the rich GATT (General Agreement on Tariffs and Trade) Members did not lend their support to the establishment of UNCTAD as they thought that it would be a

---

[22]Walt W Rostow, *The Stages of Economic Growth: A Non-Communist Manifesto*, Cambridge, Cambridge University Press (1960).
[23]The Commission on International Development was chaired by Mr Lester B Pearson. Summaries of its principal findings were published by the UNESCO Courier in February 1970 as 'Partners in Development – The Pearson Report – A New Strategy for Development'.

rival organisation to GATT; hence the word 'Conference' in the title of the organisation.[24] However, it is still surviving and surviving well.

A few other institutions established under the auspices of the UN or the World Bank for providing loans or aid and training in industries should also be mentioned in this context. The UNDP (UN Development Programme) and the UNIDO (UN Industrial Development Organisation). Aid or other forms of finance would be essential for development work, but as stated earlier that only financial help would not contribute to achieving development.

On the other hand, based on the belief that finance in its various forms, including insurance protection, should be extended to developing countries to achieve development, the International Bank for Reconstruction and Development also started extending its base by establishing the International Development Association (IDA) in 1960, the Heavily Indebted Poor Countries' Fund in 1996 and the Multilateral Investment Guarantee Agency (MIGA) in 1985. MIGA has been successful so to say; whereas IDA is merely for providing financial support to developing countries in the form of credits, the latter financially helps to keep the creditworthiness of a country, if of course, necessary, and/or if eligible for such help. In the context of this work, there is little point in going into details of these institutions. Suffice to say, that except MIGA which is basically a provider of guarantees to private foreign investors, in the event of their losing their financial investment in an eligible poor country it might be otherwise difficult for such investors to have any losses reimbursed.[25]

Based on the above discussion, it may be summarised that although after the Second World War, de-colonisation of the former colonies proved to be inevitable, it also brought in certain difficult problems. The right to self-determination prompted the colonies to attain their independence, but none of the former colonies had any effective preparation for handling their independence.[26] The euphoria of independence from the colonial masters had a blinding effect too on them.

Interestingly enough, most of the newly-born States aspired to become Westernised; without realising that each of them lacked not only the capacity but also any effective forward-looking plans. Furthermore, most of them preferred to copy their colonial power. This should be regarded as a colonial legacy.

Modernisation theory, which was inspired by Rostow, suited the euphoria of the newly-born States. Soon after the de-colonisation process started, it gained grounds, but the leaders of these countries failed to appreciate that their countries lacked the infrastructure that would be needed for modernisation. Nevertheless, these countries were provided with aid from various sources and/or borrowed

---

[24]S K Chatterjee, 'Forty Years of International Action for Trade Liberalisation', 23 *Journal of World Trade* (1992).

[25]See further S K Chatterjee, 'The Convention Establishing the Multilateral Investment Guarantee Agency', 36 *International and Comparative Law Quarterly* (1987).

[26]It was only in 1960 that the UN General Assembly adopted the Declaration on the Granting of Independence to Colonial Countries and Peoples. This Declaration was adopted on 14 December 1960 (Res. 1514 (xv)).

funds from other States or international organisations, only to increase their debt burden; modernisation had to take a back-seat.

Might collaboration between developing countries contribute to the development process bearing in mind that each developing country is different not only from their geographic and historical variations but also from the point of view of their needs and resources, both natural and human.[27] The idea of collaboration was conceived by David Mitrany, who conceptualised and promoted functionalism, believing that any successful collaboration in one area of activity would lead to further collaboration in other related areas of activity. His belief in functionalism was based on the collaborative work in the areas of transportation and communication.[28] Mitrany's idea of 'Functionalism' though sounded attractive, failed to take into consideration the problems inherent in developing countries. There do not exist many examples of inter-State collaborations, other than the ASEAN (Association of the Southeast Asian Nations) which is primarily for inter-State trade and investment, but not for socio-economic development in a country unless one argues that the spill-over effect of these activities would add to the development process in a member State. Mitrany's examples of collaboration of States in regard to transportation and communication are obvious examples in that whether or not any collaboration arrangement has been made among the parties concerned, it is in the interest of all the parties concerned that these two industries are internationalised to cover as many geographic areas as possible. This happened a very long time ago.

Along with Mahbub Ul Haq's work entitled *The Poverty Curtain: Choices for the Third World* one should also read Dudley Seer's work on Development, which he published in the form of an article entitled '*The Meaning of Development*' in which he promoted the idea that development should be considered as a social phenomenon, rather than a capital investment activity for economic growth. Seers and Haq rightly pointed out that development should not be concerned mainly with economic growth; it is a social phenomenon. This work maintains that development should represent socio-economic growth, and that economic development is not only a misleading term but also a narrow term to represent socio-economic development.[29,30]

In this context, one should reflect on the socio-economic development so far achieved by the vast majority of de-colonised countries even though majority of them attained their independence about five decades ago. In the following sections, an attempt has been made to examine among other issues the role of

---

[27]D Mitrany, 'The Functional Approach to World Organisation', 24 *International Affairs* (1948) issue 3, at 350–363.

[28]D Mitrany, 'A Political Theory for the New Society', in *Functionalism*, by AJR Groom and P Taylor, London, University of London Press (1975), at 25–38.

[29]M Ul Haq, *The Poverty Curtain: Choices for the Third World*, New York, Columbia University Press (1976).

[30]D Seers, 'The Total Relationship' in Dudley Seers and Leonard Joy (eds) *Development in a Divided World*, Baltimore, Penguin Books (1971), at 339.

governments in a development process, whether the State may be an obstacle to development, or whether it may be an enabling institution for development.

2.5 What Should Be the Role of a Government in a Development Process?

The above question is important in that most of the countries, irrespective of whether they follow a socialist or a capitalist philosophy of economy, during the early days of de-colonisation process, some of the newly-born countries wanted to opt for a socialist form of government and economy too; on the other hand, majority of the de-colonised countries seem to have opted for capitalism. However, in the final analysis, the differences in the choices of the type of government did not make much difference. The nature of a socialist government is known to almost everybody; it primarily maintains a command structure. Majority of the governments in the de-colonised countries should maintain a non-command structure, whereby peoples' participation in the governance system should be possible; indeed, the national constitutions of these countries provide for their peoples' rights and duties.

It is imperative that the government of a State should have its first duty towards its own country and peoples therein. It is reiterated that almost each of the developing countries is full of resources. Furthermore, often they have been under the control and direction of the economically stronger countries. Thus, in a way, all the developing countries seem to be sailing in similar boats.

It has already been explained that it is for the government of a State to provide health, education, capacity building in order to encourage its peoples to work for their country; when a government fails to do so, the people and their country remain backward with all the symptoms of a poor country.

After about seven decades of de-colonisation, there is hardly any point in criticising colonial legacies. The newly-born countries' aspirations for a quick modernisation was an ill thought-out aspiration, like each human body, each country's geography, circumstances and capability would be different. It is reiterated that 'development' must be achieved primarily by the indigenous people, with certain capacity-building, but during the initial period of development, with foreign experts, where necessary. That has not happened in full satisfaction, as yet. Gradually and eventually, indigenous people lose their confidence and faith in their government, and the country may eventually be dictated by a financially and militarily strong foreign power, which process would amount to having a second version of colonisation, which should be avoided by all means, but in this regard the governmental administrations have either failed their peoples or they surrendered to their chosen foreign power.

2.6 Whether a State Itself May Be an Obstacle to Development

What Abraham Lincoln said a long time ago in regard to an ideal government – 'a government of the people, by the people and for the people' is still true for all non-socialist countries. What is worrying however is that the so-called non-socialist countries, in general, seem to have adopted a hierarchical command structure for their governance. Thus, effectively, in those countries the differences between the two methods of governance become minimal. Therefore, unless peoples' participation in a governance system becomes operational, their rights and freedoms in a country are recognised and implemented, the State would act as an obstacle to development. Without an appropriate governmental support and planning, no developing country may be engaged in any development work, unless any benevolent organisation in the country concerned becomes engaged in such activity. Any premature industrialisation of a developing country, which most governments would aspire, has already been proved to be a mistake, as the vast majority of the developing countries have large agricultural sectors. Therefore, it would be logical for each such country to develop their agricultural sector and become major exporting countries after, of course, meeting their own needs for agricultural products. Industrialisation may be conducted in a slow pace, at least initially, according to the capacity of the workers. But, of course, as has been explained in this work that in this process, emphasis should be given to rural areas and their involvement in the process should contribute to 'capacity building' too.

Here, one may find it useful to reflect on two situations: those in (a) the former Soviet Union and (b) Argentina. Soon after the socialist revolution ended in 1917, the Soviet Union started its own development plan which was, in fact, rooted in Marxism, that is, a self-reliant State-based economy. Such an economy would be totally State-controlled, but eventually, it would be turned into a communist institution. Under such a regime, the peoples' participation in policy-making or whatever would not be permissible; they will be mere workers. All parts or aspects of the economy would be State-controlled, an enemy to the *Laissez-faire* doctrine. Even resources would be allocated by State authorities.[31]

Under such a regime, import tariffs are usually high; the aim is to ensure that all productions, both agricultural and industrial, are made by the employees of the regime. The assumptions on which this form of common economy is based is that this process would eventually create an egalitarian society, full employment, all citizens would enjoy an equal distribution of resources. Indeed, until the early 1970s, the Soviet economy's pace of economic progress was extremely remarkable, and most of the symptoms of a developed economy, including industrialisation, military strengths including its capability to supply military-related products and weapons, made it a matter of jealousy for many others in the world. But little did the country realise that soon she would lose her economic peak and that she would encounter a crisis; indeed, as from the latter part of the 1970s, the Soviet economy experienced a severe economic crisis combined with a massive degree of inefficiencies in various sectors of the economy.

But, as stated earlier, the Soviet economic boom in the early 1970s attracted many of the newly-born countries, but unfortunately, those countries' economy

---

[31]See further D Yergin and J Stanislaw, *The Commanding Heights – The Battle for the World Economy*, New York, Simon and Schuster (2002).

failed to achieve any appreciable socio-economic development. In this context, it would be appropriate to refer to the work of Hans Singer, which was subsequently followed up by Raul Prebisch, an Argentinian economist.[32] Singer's main theory was that the terms of trade between basic agricultural commodities and manufactured goods would deteriorate over a period of time, in consequence of which poor countries that are not exporters of agricultural products would import low-grade manufactured goods from various foreign countries.

Until about the 1920s, Argentina had a very prosperous economy, although primarily an agricultural country. Unfortunately, during the 1930s Argentina became a victim of Great Depression, and her enviable position in the world of transnational trade radically changed, and a number of Western States recommended and indeed effected subsidies for the Argentinian farmers, which further deteriorated their terms of trade for agricultural products. Argentinian agricultural market was predominantly hit by the United States and its farmers started to export subsidised wheat and beef to Argentina.

According to Prebisch, import–export trade relations between countries should not be dominated by economically and technologically superior States as this practice makes the lesser countries dependent upon those countries. It is appreciated that the primary objective of any business, in the proper sense of the term, is to make profits; but dumping of products in any developing jurisdiction at a subsidised price simply makes the recipient country dependent upon the exporting country. Rather than indirectly providing this kind of financial help which in the end will have a jeopardising effect on the recipient countries; richer and technologically advanced countries should provide technical and technological knowledge to developing countries in both agricultural and industrial sectors in order to ensure that those countries also become gradually developed in these sectors. Prebisch was very mindful of the stark differences between the structures of the developed and developing economies. It would be for public bodies concerned to deal with the issue of structural differences between the rich and the poor countries.

Prebisch suggested an Import Substitution Industrialisation (ISI) policy whereby domestic level of production would substitute foreign imports and a State-led industrialisation policy would be put into practice.

The ISI policy worked very well during its initial period of its operation in Latin America; economic growth took place especially through domestic investment in the manufacturing sector. The result of this policy was initially very encouraging in that it increased the levels of production and employment and as a necessary consequence, it also increased the national savings; but, unfortunately, it was a short-lived phenomenon in Latin America.

The debt-burden for the governments rose very fast, unemployment level also rose high; the validity of the ISI model was questioned. The dependency of the Latin American countries on foreign economies deepened. Whereas irrespective

---

[32]Raul Prebisch, *The Economic Development of Latin America and its Principal Problems*, New York, United Nations (1950).

of whether ISI model worked on the Latin American countries or not, one should not disregard the fact that without 'capacity building' knowledge in infrastructural development, it would be difficult for 'Starters' so to say, to contribute much to a development process. Based on the examples of Argentina and other Latin American countries, it may be maintained that without a non-economic infrastructure, such as, education, health, intellectual development, socio-economic development in the popular sense of the term may not be achieved.

Furthermore, as the vast majority of the developing countries that have a large agricultural sector, which includes other connected industries, such as irrigation and cottage industries, should be developed first, low- to medium-grade industries should also be developed. This is another way of enriching the rural areas in a country too. In addition, this should be another way of avoiding dependency on rich countries.

About two decades ago, Samir Amin, a Marxist economist, who advocated self-reliance of the newly-born countries, which it is maintained, would be the most preferable means of developing the economies of the newly-born countries. However, Amin's work was based on Lenin's theory of imperialism, who argued that capitalism had an expansionist philosophy, in consequence of which it would attempt to establish monopolies in poor countries, particularly for obtaining their natural resources, and based on Prebisch's idea perhaps, like it happened in Argentina and other Latin American countries, the capitalist West would capture the markets for agricultural products by dumping their subsidised agricultural products too.[33] But from a realistic point of view, one may raise the question whether the newly-born countries should totally isolate themselves from the wealthy and inventive West, bearing in mind that the Marxist theories of development became rather obsolete with the demise of the Soviet Union in 1991. On the other hand, without taking any sides in favour of or against capitalism and socialism, one may raise the question what would be the best method of achieving socio-economic development by the newly-born countries, in general?

Before going into any details of what the newly-born countries, in general, should do, it may be apposite to reiterate that the governments of these countries should not think of any dependency on any country, which would invite another version of colonialism; secondly, each developing country being different, governments should assess their own capabilities, particularly with reference to their strength in the following sectors in particular, agriculture, natural resources and human resources. Most of the developing countries tend to depend on foreign aid of different forms and expect their former colonial powers to come to their rescue. Thus, there hardly exists any novel ideas. Their own independent status is again relegated to a status of dependency. Most importantly, their judiciary is, in general, considered to be unreliable and biased. Thus, States themselves may in certain cases be regarded as an obstacle to development.

---

[33]S Amin, *Obsolescent Capitalism: Contemporary Politics and Global Disorder*, London, Zed Books (2003).

2.7 Whether a State May Be an Enabling Institution for Development

From a theoretical perspective, there is no reason why a State may not be an enabling institution for development, but the reality seems to be different. In this context, one should perhaps consider the principle of sovereignty which has often been abused by States. The meaning of the term 'Sovereignty' is 'Omnipotence' – all 'powerful'. This is where the problem starts. The idea of being 'all powerful' provides a sense of 'ego' which may eventually mature into an authoritarian power. This is also the source of adopting a hierarchical command structure, whereas a non-hierarchical command structure will usually have a governance system based on peoples' participation – a fundamental trait of a democratic governance system. But, in a formal democratic governance system, it is quite possible to operate a pseudo-democratic system. Examples of this form of system are in abundance. There however does not exist any perfect democracy; so, it is a question of the degree of participation of the peoples' representation allowed by the government. Most of the newly-born countries seem to be operating a pseudo-democratic governance system.

The UNDP (the UN Development Programmes), which has been a supporter of human development, published its Report entitled *Human Development for Everyone*, 2016 but unfortunately, most of the Members of the UN tend to disregard its guidelines or even resolutions on the grounds that they are not binding, without appreciating that it cannot work as a Sovereign of Sovereign States; however, its principal function is to offer guidelines to its Member States.[34]

The high flow of emigration over the last decades from many of the developing countries to many of the developed countries is an indication of the frustration of the immigrants in the political condition in their countries, which ideally should not have happened. Instead of dealing with the popular expression of 'poverty trap', Paul Collier maintained that the poor countries are not necessarily in a poverty trap; on the contrary, he devised various traps for them, one of them being bad governance.[35] It has already been explained when a governance is a bad governance, or it should be changed.

More recently, Professor A Sen, who was awarded Nobel Prize in Economics in 1998, promoted in his work entitled, *Development as Freedom*, the idea of human freedoms as an important factor of development.[36] He also advocated the role of women and minorities in a development process. Professor Sen's idea of human freedom as a factor of development is noteworthy in that he has been an ardent supporter of human development rather than emphasising the importance

---

[34]UNDP, *Human Development Report 2016: Human Development for Everyone*, New York, UNDP.

[35]P Collier, *The Bottom Billion: Why the Poorest Countries Are Failing and What Can Be Done About It*, Oxford, Oxford University Press (2008), at 5.

[36]A Sen, *Development as Freedom*, New York, Random House (1999).

of capital investments, foreign aids, etc.[37] Sen also categorised the types of human freedoms, which in his opinion, would add to a development process:

- Political freedom – this would include, for example, freedom to form opposition against the government in power and/or force elections;
- Social opportunities – this would include, for example, access to health care and education;
- Economic opportunities – a version of *Laissez-faire* doctrine, and of course, the capability to get employment;
- Guarantees of transparency from the government in power; and
- Protective security – such as governmental benefits to unemployed or protection of the rights of people.

These freedoms, opportunities, securities and guarantees, as identified by Sen, are or should be made available by all non-dictatorial governments, but as explained before that the vast majority of the governments of the developing countries do, in reality, maintain, in effect, a command structure, which runs counter to a non-dictatorial governance system. This is one of the most important reasons why the vast majority of developing countries remain so.

However, in a non-dictatorial system of governance, people should be reminded of their duties to their country and communities. It may be maintained that this is particularly important for the newly-born countries in their attempts to achieving their socio-economic development.

In his work, Sen also mentioned that under a protective security system, the rule of law, which should be regarded as an extremely important means of protecting the fundamental rights and freedoms of peoples in a country. In the event of a breach of these, the injured party must have direct access to seek his/her remedies from an impartial judiciary. An impartial judicial system may only be achieved if it is entirely separable and separate from the executive authorities in a country.

Interestingly enough, even the vast majority of the developed countries, let alone the developing countries, do not operate this system in an ideal manner, although it may be maintained that by making their judiciary entirely separable and separate from their executive authorities, they may not be able to maintain an impartial judiciary. But, at the same time, it is important to see that a judiciary in a country is not only impartial from a functional point of view but also organically separable and separate from their executive authorities.

In England including Wales, despite the fact that judges are appointed by the Constitutional Department of the government with the recommendation of the Lord Chancellor, and their salaries come from a government fund, the judiciary has an enviable reputation of being impartial.[38] Indeed, being primarily a

---

[37]See also W Easterly, *The Tyranny of Experts: Economists, Dictators and the Forgotten Rights of the Poor*, New York, Basic Books (2013).

[38]Scotland's judicial system is separate from the English judicial system; Northern Ireland has also their separate judicial system, but they share the same Supreme Court with England and Wales.

remedial system, even individuals will have access to the relevant courts irrespective of whether they have the capacity to engage representatives (e.g. solicitors and/or barristers or King's Counsels) to act on their behalf, unless of course, on the basis of the merits of each case, they have been granted legal aid by the National Legal Aid fund which is currently distributed to eligible solicitors' firms.

In view of the English judiciary's enviable reputation of being entirely impartial, foreign parties, in the event of their successfully establishing any link to the English jurisdiction usually refer their disputes, particularly those having a commercial dimension (e.g. banking, private foreign investment, shipping, trade, etc.) to the English judiciary.

An effective system of providing protection to the individual of his/her rights and freedom must be regarded as an integral part of an enviable socio-economic system.

2.8 Conclusions

In the brief literature review, it has been clear that none of the eminent authors whose works have been referred to, defined the term 'development'; on the contrary, majority of them gave their considered views how 'development' according to their respective theory or perception may be achieved. Some of such views are worth considering, but in the final analysis, there does not exist any united view on what 'development' may stand for. On the other hand, from a pragmatic standpoint, it might not be appropriate to devise any specific definition of 'development' as the needs for and availability of resources in each country are different; nevertheless, the common element of all development processes would be that they must be participatory, and where possible, should be achieved through indigenous means. Each development process must ensure 'capacity building' of the indigenous people.

Sen and subsequently Easterly supported human development as an important factor of development, which would lead to peoples' freedom, an essential component of democracy – the elements of which Sen identified.

After the de-colonisation process started, the majority of the de-colonised countries seem to have visualised their own development through the eyes of the Western world. This is where, it is maintained, that things started to go wrong. Until about the early part of the 1980s, a technology-based development was viewed by many authors and politicians as the major means of developing an economy without appreciating that the newly-born countries would not be able to compete with the Western world on this issue unless some exceptions take place, such as India or Singapore.

Furthermore, the vast majority of the de-colonised countries have primarily an agricultural economy; the agricultural sectors in these countries should have been made sophisticated and the very large rural areas where the majority of the people live, and where also agricultural land areas are available should have been looked after well. As stated earlier, the vast majority of these countries are poor.

Thus, the concept of 'development' primarily remained mostly as an academic idea which was basically philosophically charged, without reaching an effective and appropriate diagnosis for the cure of poverty. Meanwhile, the majority of the newly-born countries were led by leaders who, in the main, depended on the expertise and finance of the developed West. Two issues should be reiterated in this context: (a) to what extent the West from which the vast majority of the colonial powers originated, were similar to the colonised areas, even though by virtue of being colonial powers they had a degree of familiarity with their colonies and (b) the colonised people being dominated by their colonial powers and after the de-colonisation process started, in most cases were dominated by their own political structure. With the exception of a limited number of countries, namely, Bolivia, Brazil, India, Pakistan and South Africa, in which certain political leaders launched movements of independence, in the vast majority of the former colonies, people surrendered themselves to servitude and aspired to follow the life style of the Western people, where possible.

Sen's work – *Development as Freedom*, was the first work to import the idea of 'human-centred development' rather than technology-based development. However, without being overcritical of his work, if one had reversed the title of his work to say 'Freedom is Development', would it have been more appropriate to signify what 'development' really stood for in reality? If people in a developing country had been allowed their rights and freedoms, including their right to education, training (capacity building), health and indeed, seek remedies for an impartial judiciary in the event of their freedom and rights being denied, would the 'development process' in a country have been much more people-oriented and the people in the rural areas could have been easily motivated to undertake development work in their own interests? Those of the developing countries that have already proceeded in this direction deserve credit.

On this issue, one may like to re-visit Hayek, who was an ardent supporter of free markets, and yet believed that the State had a role to play as a regulatory institution. This is what determines the scope of activities of governments too. They should not be dictatorial, but they will have the right to enforce any breach of legislation. By the same token, peoples' government is a theoretical aspiration; it is not implementable. Instead, governments should be participatory which means that it must contain participation of the chosen members of the community. This system should raise the level of public awareness and lift the level of encouragement among people in a society to work for their country (through various projects).

Chapter 3

Hindrances to Rural Development

Abstract

This is an elementary and yet important chapter. In this chapter, the most important hindrances to rural development have been identified and how they usually hinder development has been explained. Various forms of bias that adversely affect a rural development process, namely, spatial bias, person bias, elite bias, male bias, user and adopter bias, and active present and living biases have also been briefly discussed.

Keywords: Bias; hindrances; farming; finance; knowledge

3.1 Introduction

Rural development can be an instrument of eradicating poverty in the rural areas of a country. In developing this work, it has already been suggested that in view of the benefits attached to rural marketing, rural development may be achieved faster and constructively with the participation of the people in the rural area concerned as they should know their part of the area best.

In this chapter an attempt is made to identify some of the important issues, not all, of course, which seem to hinder rural development and as a consequence, promote rural poverty. Interestingly enough, it is often the urban people and institutions in the urban areas that seem to neglect the rural areas in their country, in consequence of which the central government or the state government, as the case may be, does not feel pressurised to go into their rural areas. The causes of poverty are numerous, but the neglect of rural areas by people and institutions working in urban areas significantly contribute to it too.

There is no need to describe the miseries of poverty in rural areas – they are simply abject. There also exists a high degree of 'prejudice' on the part of urban people against people living in rural areas. In the majority of cases, given the fact that rural areas in a country are usually larger than urban areas, the financial resources made available to rural areas for socio-economic development are not

Rural Marketing as a Tool for National Development, 41–49

Copyright © 2024 Charles Chatterjee

Published under exclusive licence by Emerald Publishing Limited

doi:10.1108/978-1-83608-064-020241004

abundant compared to their needs. Furthermore, growth of industries and educational facilities for rural people remain insignificant. Rural people remain less knowledgeable and less technology-oriented.

On the other hand, doubts exist as to whether urban people would understand the rural areas in their part of the country. They are outsiders. By analogy, this has proved to be one of the major problems in achieving socio-economic development in developing countries by outsiders – the foreign developers who may not have much idea of the developing country concerned. This is one of the reasons why this work recommends rural development with the participation of rural people. If developers suffer from certain pre-conceived ideas and engage themselves in development work with a sense of 'pity' for the deserving people, then development may not be achieved. Furthermore, outsiders are often reluctant to know the nature of the rural problems in any country, which are so deep-rooted.[1] Mere short visits by outsiders, including urban professionals, will not make them sufficiently familiar with rural problems. By the same token, rural people, if asked to develop urban areas may be criticised on similar grounds.

In this chapter, an attempt is made to examine the best means of identifying who may be the best actors for achieving socio-economic development in rural areas, and whether outsiders, who may be needed for this kind of venture, may be made fully knowledgeable in rural issues and problems. Thus, the next question arises – the extent to which rural development may be achieved solely through the participation of the rural people.

In the context of this work, it is important to emphasise that one should aim at socio-economic development rather than economic development as the former expression includes development of education, training, health, etc. (the factors that are essential for social well-being); a country may be financially wealthy but may not have achieved social well-being of her people.

3.2 What Role May Outsiders Be Allowed to Take for Achieving Socio-Economic Development in a Rural Area?

'Outsiders' in this context would include not only the urban people in a country of which the rural areas are part but also foreigners, including foreign corporate entities and aid providers. These people and organisations are described as 'outsiders' simply because they are not usually familiar with the real rural conditions, the rural people, and the real needs of these people, by virtue of not being inhabitants in these areas. These people and institutions may not be familiar with the way of life of the rural people, their attitudes towards life and their ambitions. It is important to bear in mind that in the name of 'rural development' they must not impose on them straightaway the style of life of urban people, as consideration should be given to the fact that these areas lack appropriate infrastructures

---

[1]See further R Chambers, *Rural Development: Putting the Last First*, Harlow, Prentice Hall (1983) at 3, 4

and educational facilities. Additionally, the majority of the people either depend on the agricultural sector or a very primitive form of small industries.

Incidentally, outsiders should not take the role of 'do-gooders' as in most cases they may not be aware of the processes and stages of introducing 'good things' to rural people. The final aim of rural development would be to transform them into urban areas with most of the facilities, which are traditionally available in those areas but not destroying the good aspects of 'rural life'. This balance may be difficult to strike by outsiders; hence the need for consultation with and involvement of rural people in achieving rural development. It may be beneficial for the urban people in the country of which the rural areas are part, to inform themselves of the aspirations of the rural people – their language, their way of life, etc. As stated earlier that gradually and eventually the rural areas would hopefully be transformed into urban areas; but the 'ruralness' of the areas should not be destroyed. Industrialisation of the rural areas would be necessary but not at the cost of environmental pollution or health hazards. In the development process, the outsiders should pay their most attention to education, training and skills development for the rural people.

The other 'outsiders' in this context would be the urban people from the relevant government entities who, in the event of a country being a recipient of aid from a truly international organisation, namely, International Development Agency (IDA) under the World Bank Group or a non-governmental organisation, such as the Christian Aid or Oxfam. These organisations usually visit these areas for a short while to arrange only the administrative aspects of the aid allowed through the intervention of the recipient government. Incidentally, the term 'aid' has two meanings: (a) financial aid for a short period of time and (b) to provide the rural areas training instead of providing money. In the event of 'training' a full bi-lateral understanding must be developed between the two parties concerned.

Although these firms are outsiders, with direct interaction with the local rural employees, they will be informed of the choices, needs and the style of the rural way of living much more quickly than the others provided they are able to communicate through a common language. They will also have the advantage of visiting the strategically important locations in the rural area concerned, as often as necessary. Only positive interactions with rural people in a simple language should generate business interests for both the parties – the providers of knowledge, skills and training and the recipients of these. This must be regarded as one of the most important factors of socio-economic development in rural areas. Rural development should be through the local rural people with the aid of training of informed outsiders, and in this process the latter will also benefit from this scheme by having goods in the production of which they may lack expertise, but the aid receiving country does not do so.

The outsiders' role in a rural development process should be that of a mentor, but not for the purpose of indoctrinating the rural participants engaged in the process, but merely to guide them to develop knowledge and skills in them to meet the development needs bearing in mind that the rural participants know the rural situations well although they may not be as articulate as their guides. They should also provide them management skills for managing the project after completion. A development process must be interesting for the recipient of development and the process must be participatory. Where possible, the outsiders should also ensure that the materials which might be necessary for the completion of a project may be obtained from the local sources; otherwise, the project may not be cost-effective. The outsiders must maintain their neutrality, must impart their knowledge and skills to the recipient fully and without any selfish motive; they must also take interest in the project so that their devotion to it may not be questioned. By such combined role of the outsiders and the rural people, the outsiders will also be knowledgeable about rural conditions and deficiencies in their areas and the nature of the people therein whereby they would gain competence in operating such projects in the future elsewhere too. The outsiders should thus be involved in projects for educational purposes, but ultimately, they will also derive benefits, financial or otherwise from such ventures.

3.3 Bias in Rural Development

As indicated before most of the developing countries tend to neglect the need for rural development either overtly or covertly, even though in most of the developing countries rural areas are larger than urban areas and that a large population live in those areas. According to Chambers, there exist seven types of bias that seem to work against rural development.

3.3.1 Spatial Bias

The fact that in the name of rural development most actors concentrate on their development work near to high roads or areas near to urban centres; this practice has been described by Chambers as spatial bias, and in support of the existence of this type of bias, he cited the example of agricultural demonstrations of new seeds and fertilisers in Tamil Nadu in India, which were often sited beside main roads. Chambers also pointed out that an improved tarmac or all-weather surface would also bring buses, telephone, electricity, better access to markets, health facilities, schools, etc. Services near main roads are better staffed and equipped. He also referred to Edward Heneveld's findings that two schools near a main highway in Sumatra had more than their permissible quota of teachers, whereas a school that was located only one mile away from the main highway could not fill in their quota of teachers.[2]

In fact, developed rural areas by the road side attract rich people to buy land and eventually will have houses built on such land areas, in consequence of which the rural people are left with no choice but to transfer themselves into more remote areas; thus rural poverty not only mobilises but also in view of the remoteness of such areas governments and developers, in general, lose interests in eradicating poverty by offering opportunities through industries or other projects in those areas where poverty precipitates.

The study carried out by Moore and Wickramasinghe on three villages in Sri Lanka also confirmed how 'hidden poverty' exists in the low areas of the country.

---

[2]Chambers, op. cit., at 13.

Their study also confirmed that wealthier people use their social and economic power to obtain roadside sites as public transport facilities, electricity and communication system are available in those areas. These authors and Chambers maintain that many visitors including public officers end up visiting these areas only rather than seeing how poverty persists in remote rural areas.[3]

Spatial bias thus hinders progress in all senses of the term in deep rural areas where poverty deepens as a result of neglect of and prejudices against deep rural areas in a country.

3.3.2 Project Bias

This type of bias stands for bias in choosing projects which may not really be very helpful for the deep rural areas. The policy-makers do not, in practice, venture in the areas which should be designated as 'priority areas'. According to Chambers,

> Project bias is most marked with the showpiece: the nicely groomed pet project or model village, specially staffed and supported, with well briefed members who know what to say and which is sited a reasonable but not excessive distance from the urban headquarters.[4]

These projects are really for pleasing the tourists or other types of visitors. The authorities in the country concerned 'divert their attention from the poorer people'.[5]

In support of his argument about project bias, Chambers cited examples of certain projects in developing countries, namely, Chile Agricultural Development Unit in Ethiopia; the Comilla Project in Bangladesh; the Gezira Scheme in Sudan; and the Mwea Irrigation Settlement in Kenya. But none of these projects was undertaken in the very rural parts of the country concerned. The question therefore remains whether projects in the peripheries of cities or large towns would really help eradicate poverty in the distant rural areas where the poor people tend to live.

3.3.3 Person Bias

Person bias stands for bias in favour or against a person. Chambers maintained that rural development tourists, local level officials or rural researchers are usually provided by those who are biased against poorer people. An analysis of this opinion would suggest that indigenous people may present a difficult hurdle to real rural development.

---

[3]See further M P Moore and G Wickramasinghe, *Agriculture and Society in the Low Country (Sri Lanka)*, Agrarian Research and Training Institute, Colombo 1980, and Chambers, op. cit.

[4]R Chambers, op. cit., at 16.

[5]Ibid.

Chambers then divides bias into four categories: (i) Elite bias; (ii) Male bias, (iii) User and Adopter biases; and (iv) Active, Present and Living biases. These are now briefly addressed.

3.3.4 Elite Bias

This form of bias relates to those rural people who have influence over the rural area concerned and who are less poor compared to the others in the same geographical area. These people are typically more successful farmers, teachers, religious leaders; in other words, these categories of people are more influential than the majority and they often represent their village to the foreign people and visitors. Thus, the real poor people are not allowed to represent their village in consequence of which the visitors do not receive the real information on rural areas. From a psychological standpoint, the poor feel powerless, short of information, and perhaps inarticulate; thus, they feel themselves incapable of presenting their ideas about their village. According to Devitt,

> The poor are often inconspicuous, inarticulate and unorganised. Their voices may not be heard at public meetings in communities where it is customary for only the big men to put their views... Outsiders and government officials invariably find it more profitable and congenial to converse with local influential than with the uncommunicative poor.[6]

Thus, the real conditions of the poor in the inner rural areas remain unknown to the outsiders.

3.3.5 Male Bias

In developing countries, in general, villages are male-dominated, particularly in response of management of land, or any private foreign investments. Females, whether as housewives or workers are dominated by males, which has been a practice for a very long time. Of course, this situation has significantly changed in urban areas primarily because of opportunities for females to pursue higher education, which lead to their obtaining good positions in both public and private sectors. Within rural areas, in general, male bias is not based on their enlightenment but more of a tradition in many developing countries. But it is through development of the rural areas that this situation might be changed.

---

[6]P Devitt, 'Notes on Poverty-oriented Rural Development', in Extension, Planning and the poor, Agricultural Administration Unit Occasional Paper, Overseas Development Institute (1977) at 23.

3.3.6 User and Adopter Bias

Where rural visits are arranged for visitors, particularly, foreign visitors, according to Chambers, primarily, if not exclusively, the users of services and the adopters of new practices are more likely to be seen in those areas than non-users of facilities and non-adopters of new practices.[7] Obviously, the visitors feel themselves very assured of the rural development initiated by the government concerned. Visitors will have no knowledge of how many non-users of the facilities and new innovations exist, nor would they have any information, for example, on how many children do not have the privilege of having school education. What is needed is by legislation, education of children up to the secondary level, should be made compulsory and funded by the government and under an effective enforcement procedure. Private education should be limited to those who are able to afford it; however, there should not be any discrimination between those who have had their education at government funded schools and those of the children/young people who have had it at private schools.

3.3.7 Active, Present and Living Biases

Under this category of bias, Chambers maintained that when some new events take place, whether by virtue of the appearance of new visitors or whatever only the healthy and happy children come out and enjoy themselves, whereas the poor, unhealthy and so many ill children stay home. Furthermore, he referred to Turnbull's experience in Uganda, where he described how he spent time camping outside a village there, before he realised that old people were starving.[8] Much of the rural poverty and miseries remain in the dark.

3.4 Governmental Politics and Bias

This type of bias is rather all pervasive in the majority of the developing countries, whereby the ruling government deters foreign visitors to see the real nature of poverty in the remote rural areas in a developing country, presumably in order to avoid adverse publicity of poverty in the country. Furthermore, from a psychological point of view, the government will feel a degree of shame in showing the visitors any signs of abject poverty, as it has a direct impact on its poverty-reduction policy. Chambers has designated this type of bias as 'Diplomatic biases: politeness and timidity'.[9] It is interesting to note that in most cases, successive governments follow the same footprints of their predecessors in this regard. In other words, again the voice of the rural people in development efforts, if any, remain unheard and as stated earlier that vast amount of human resources remains unutilised in these countries.

---

[7] R Chambers, op. cit., at 19.
[8] C Turnbull, *The Mountain People*, London, Picador, Pan Books (1973) at 102.
[9] R Chambers, op. cit., at 22.

3.5 Professional Biases

In discussing this form of bias, Chambers pointed out, inter alia, that:

> ... professionals in rural areas become even more narrowly single-minded. They do their own thing and only their own thing. They look for and find what fits their ideas. There is neither inclination nor time for the open-ended question or for other ways of perceiving people, events and things.[10]

Governments in developing countries may like to follow the examples of rural development process and programmes in developed countries which were also at similar stages. But, in developing countries, in general, rural development seems to be often hindered for the biases explained above.

3.6 Conclusions

The primary objective of this chapter was to establish the human prejudices, including governmental prejudices in certain cases, which seem to be responsible for subjecting the residents in remote village areas in developing countries, to abject poverty without creating any opportunities whereby they would be able to learn skills and gain knowledge. The foreign tourists will not have any chance to witness the conditions in which the villagers really live. This issue has been clearly identified and explained by Professor Chambers in his work, which has often been referred to in this chapter.

Developing countries, in general, should now appreciate that socio-economic development in a country must come from within, and that only with relevant foreign assistance, where necessary, their peoples' capacity should be built. Only foreign aid for developmental purposes will not do; although foreign aid may be necessary for socio-economic development in certain special cases, they must also appreciate that aid has a darker side too – it simply increases the burden of dependency in consequence of which they lose their voice and reputation at international fora, unless the 'aid' is used for training of the local people, and that its terms and conditions of re-payment by any alternative means have been written in the relevant contract.

It is important to bear in mind that the indigenous and local people know better than any overseas agencies or individuals what they need and how their development should be achieved without distorting their own way of life. But, of course, there are certain businesses, namely, banking, insurance, shipping, etc to name but a few, where Western expertise may be necessary as they are advanced in these business areas. Thus, it would be worthwhile to discuss the development of these industries/businesses with a view to informing themselves (the developing countries' leaders) how they may like to develop those industries to cater for their

---

[10]R Chambers, op. cit., at 23.

own people first, and thereafter to raise the standards of those industries/ businesses to a level which would match the expectation of some of the people in the West involved in those businesses.

It is quite possible for developing countries to diversify their economies through well thought-out planning and the appropriate utilisation of their human resources rather than neglecting them. This is another reason why this work advocates 'marketing' as a platform for providing skills and knowledge to the rural people, particularly those who live in the remote villages.

One of the perennial problems which cuts across the developing countries, in general, is that the tenets of democracy are hardly implemented, and this has proved to be a predictable phenomenon in many countries in that part of the world. This is counter-productive in their own interests. Furthermore, private foreign investors (otherwise known as transnational corporations) show their reluctance to invest in those countries. This situation is further aggravated by the lack of reliable investment policies, and investors' protection systems, screening policies, etc. Private foreign investors would like to see that these risks are eliminated and that they also have continuity in their investment policies with a view to developing confidence in their minds, in addition to developing reliable administrative and judicial systems.

These are all integral parts of a socio-economic development process. Ministerial changes are inevitable in all governments, but the continuity and improvement of policies which might otherwise adversely affect the interests of not only the nationals and residents but also the private foreign investors are one of the functions of the expert bureaucrats who are not usually changed with the entry of a new political administration.

Socio-economic development process in developing countries may not necessarily be modelled on that generally adopted by the Western world. If one closely looks at the principal urban areas in developing countries, they have been largely modelled on Western countries at the cost of the developing countries' own philosophies and way of life. What they seem to have forgotten is that the rural areas in the developed world are also developed in the proper sense of the term.

Chapter 4

Regulatory Measures Required for Rural Marketing and Sales

Abstract

In this chapter, the most important regulatory measures required for rural marketing and sales have been identified – why protection of consumers' interests should be maintained; why rural development is important; the role of Code of Conduct, particularly on Advertising and Marketing Communication Practice 2011, and the role of Codes, in general, but in particular, International Code of Advertising Practice 1986, the Code of Marketing Practice, the International Code of Sales Promotion 1987, etc. have received attention.

Keywords: Regulatory; measures; consumers; interests; codes

4.1 Introduction

In carrying out marketing and sales activities, regulatory measures for protecting the interests of sellers and buyers are essential. In this respect, there is hardly any point in following the regulatory measures adopted and implemented by the Western world, although they often vary from country to country within the Western world. Nevertheless, all countries, developed or developing, should be mindful of consumer protection; any derogation from it will have a counter-productive effect on sellers and suppliers of products and services.

Of course, regulatory measures must be such which may be effectively endorsed by the State concerned. This will of course need well-trained enforcement officers, which essential may not be satisfied by many countries as yet. In order to minimise the incidence of protection for consumers in any country, particularly in the rural areas, the level of public awareness and education have to be raised, which are currently not so appreciably visible in the rural areas in many countries. Nevertheless, all markets, be they urban or rural, must be regulated in accordance with the characteristics of the market concerned.

Rural Marketing as a Tool for National Development, 51–66
Copyright © 2024 Charles Chatterjee
Published under exclusive licence by Emerald Publishing Limited
doi:10.1108/978-1-83608-064-020241005

4.2 The Nature of Regulatory Measures for Protecting Consumers' Interests

In rural areas consumers are not, in general, familiar with regulatory measures primarily for two reasons: (a) that perhaps no such measures have been introduced to them and (b) that the regulatory measures may not be understood by them. This situation may be rectified by adopting two measures: (a) to introduce regulatory measures through all kinds of media, namely, television, radio, advertisements in the local language(s) and (b) by introducing to them regulatory measures in the simplest form of the local language and even by pictures and handbills. At the same time, the rural consumers should be made aware of their rights. From this standpoint, no distinction should be made between people in urban areas and rural areas. It is important to re-emphasise that in almost all countries, markets are larger in rural areas than in urban areas. Labelling and packaging of food products, in particular, should be done in compliance with WHO's (World Health Organisation) guidelines, and instructions should be made available to them in the simplest possible language. The date by which, for example, packaged food products should be consumed should be clearly indicated on the label or container, as the case may be, bearing in mind that except countries such as Mongolia, for example, the vast majority of the countries in the developing world are tropical countries; thus, food products go stale quite quickly. In rural marketing, a very high level of ethics must be maintained; this is because marketeers and sales persons must not take advantage of customers who for obvious reasons are less informed compared to urban customers.

Regulatory measures addressed exclusively to rural people would be meaningless if they are unable to understand them. Thus, these measures must be explained in the simplest possible language; often different versions of it in different languages may have to be developed. Regulatory measures must be capable of being enforced in rural areas in the event of their breach. In view of the significant differences between the rural areas in the West (which indirectly may be described as semi-urban areas) and those in developing countries, in general, the regulatory measures developed in the West should not be copied for rural areas in developing countries, although the basic ethos of the regulatory measures in the West should be looked into in developing the regulatory measures meant for rural areas in developing countries.

The theme of this work is to attain socio-economic development in developing countries through modernisation and industrialisation of the rural areas in the developing world. It has already been stated in this work that only aid-giving by foreign donors, be they institutional or otherwise, will not do. Socio-economic development must be achieved through the participation of the local people, who also must be enlightened to appreciate what they are supposed to contribute to achieving their own socio-economic development.

Rural development through marketing and sales of products will thus, in the main, entail the following:

- to raise the level of public awareness through education;
- to provide training and skills to rural people;

- to provide rural people employment;
- to raise their habit of banking;
- to raise the levels of their consumption of products;
- to set up branches of factories so that rural people can use their skills upon training; and
- to change their lifestyle.

Rural marketing would thus be a multi-dimensional phenomenon; it should extend the markets for urban industries and outlets, by setting up branches and manufacturing units in those areas. This will also offer female human resources to be utilised for remuneration. With training, females living in rural areas may take the initiative of setting up their industries with small amounts of capital. This is why it has been suggested in this work that banks should set up their branches in rural areas and extend loans to appropriate enterprises. This has already happened in India. There are no magic ways of achieving rural development, it is through multi-dimensional initiatives that rural development may be achieved in a country.

As stated earlier, the regulatory measures addressed to rural development must be developed to conform to the objectives of rural development. Rural marketing is not to be aimed at intensifying marketing and sales activities within rural areas but also to provide education and training (capacity building) to rural people to contribute to their own development process. This would also raise the level of their self-esteem.

Returning to the issue of regulatory measures to be adopted for marketing and sales in rural areas, it would be inappropriate to prescribe those measures which should be applied to all rural areas; instead, it is thought to be more appropriate to examine some of the important provisions of certain codes of conduct on marketing and sales, in general, developed by some of the prestigious non-governmental organisations. Although these are primarily addressed to the Western world, there is no reason why some of these provisions may not be applied to rural areas in developing countries too.

4.3 An Examination of Some of the Important Provisions of Certain of the Codes of Conduct Developed by Non-governmental Institutions

Although marketing and sales may be deemed to be a factor of socio-economic development, it has to be used within limits so that it does not mislead customers in any way particularly when they are not sufficiently informed of the quality of the product and whether it would be fit for the purpose. From this standpoint, the standards of ethics in doing business in rural areas should be higher than that in urban areas; however, in no circumstances would businesspeople be allowed to mislead their customers, current or prospective. Under the common law systems, they may be accused of misrepresentation of facts and also as an act of deliberate negligence.

The Codes which are about to be discussed are addressed to sellers and providers of products and services, which, as stated earlier, should also be followed by sellers and providers of products and services in the rural areas in the developing world; although they are addressed to sellers and providers of products and services, they should be a factor of enlightenment for the buyers and sellers in developing countries' markets too, which is one of the main reasons for developing this work.

4.3.1 The Consolidated ICC Code of Advertising and Marketing Communication Practice, 2011

The primary objective of this Code is to facilitate an effective implementation of the ICC Marketing Codes and similar regulatory measures adopted by the ICC. It stands for a guide which all sellers may like to follow. This Code has replaced the International Code on Advertising Practice 1986, and the Rules for the ICC (International Chamber of Commerce) International Council on Marketing Practice, 1988. This Code maintains that in implementing it, attention should be paid to the relevant culture and commercial conditions in the jurisdiction concerned. This point is particularly relevant to recent marketing practice in the developing world. By now, the majority of the developing countries have adopted a variety of legislations and regulations along the lines of the developed States, but the lack of their enforcement has remained as a debatable issue. Providers of goods and services have therefore a special responsibility that in providing goods and services they do not become unethical and take advantage of the lack of enforcement measures. This Code also emphasises the importance of education with a view to enlightening the providers of products and services so that they remain ethical in their objectives and at the same time to raise the level of knowledge in consumers; again, this point is particularly important for rural customers.[1]

In addition to an Introduction and certain General Provisions on Advertising and Marketing Communication Practice this Code has been developed over Five Chapters:

Chapter A – Sales Promotion (Articles A1 – A10);
Chapter B – Sponsorship (Articles B1 – B13);
Chapter C – Direct Marketing (Articles C1 – C17);
Chapter D – Advertising and Marketing Communications using Digital Interactive Media (Articles D1 – D8); and
Chapter E – Environmental Claims in Marketing Communications (Articles E1 – E8)

In the context of this work, there is no need to go into the details of each of these chapters; the primary idea is to refer to the most important provisions of

---

[1]This method of implementing this Code have been detailed in the Code's Annex II. https://icc.se/wp-content/uploads/2015/09/icc-consolidated-code-of-advertising-and-marketing-2011-english.pdf

them and to relate them to rural marketing. The ICC also recommended that this Code should also be read in conjunction with the other related Codes, principles and framework interpretations, namely,

- ICC International Code of Direct Marketing;
- ICC/ESCMAR International Code of Market and Social Research;
- ICC Principles on Responsible Deployment of Electronic Product Codes;
- ICC Framework for Responsible Food and Beverage Communications; and
- ICC Framework for Responsible Environmental Marketing Communications.

The Consolidated ICC Code emphasises the importance of maintaining the standards of ethical conduct which should be observed by everyone involved in marketing communications in any manner, namely, whether through the media or through advertisements or otherwise.

The above issue concerning the need for maintaining the standards of ethical conduct is particularly important for rural marketing in view of the lack of information the rural people in developing countries, in general, suffer from; it would be totally unfair and unethical to provide them untrue information on consumer products, and indeed would also be an unethical act on the part of marketeers and sellers in rural areas in developing countries bearing in mind that they are very different from the rural areas in the developed parts of the world. As stated earlier, the standards of ethics of rural marketeers and sellers must be much higher than those in urban areas as consumers in the latter areas have opportunities to inform themselves of the qualities or the lack of qualities of consumer products than consumers in the rural areas in developing countries. It is also essential to re-emphasise that the basic context of this work is to establish that rural marketing process, when operated with good intention may be a formidable platform for socio-economic development in developing countries.

This Code may be adapted to any socio-economic conditions; it may not be treated as a Code exclusively meant for developed economies. Thus, who may be regarded as a 'child', for example, may be determined by the society concerned in which this Code may have been decided to be applied. Incidentally, this is one of the reasons why this work emphasised the need for high level of public awareness and the existence of active non-governmental organisations in all countries. There are certain terms which need to be analysed in the context of rural marketing. This Code of Conduct, for obvious reasons, had referred to them in general terms.

Consumers are individuals who would consume or use a product manufactured by somebody else. Both the aspects of this definition entail responsibility on the part of the producer or manufacturer of the product, whereby neither of them should suppress anything, in particular, the weakness(es) of the product. No prior knowledge of the product including its weakness on the part of a consumer may be assumed. Indeed, in England and Wales, the traditional principle of *caveat emptor* – buyer beware – has been abolished; the sellers of products or providers of services have now the sole responsibility of explaining the features of the goods and services for the purpose of informing the prospective customer of these in order to enable him/it to reach a decision upon being informed by the seller or provider respectively of goods or services whether to acquire it for a consideration (a price). Hence, the need for transparent 'labelling' of products/services, including the life of a product by which it must be consumed, for example.

In the case of rural consumers particularly in developing countries, the language in which (sometimes in a special dialect in particular regions) the features of a product or services, including its deficiencies, must be detailed in a very simple language without using any jargon in it so that the less-educated or totally uneducated people can understand it. This is a special responsibility that rural sellers, marketeers and introducers of products and services must discharge.

According to the Consolidated ICC Code, the term 'marketing communications' includes advertising as well as other techniques, for example, promotions, direct marketing; or even attempts to 'influence consumer behaviour'. This is where the problem lies. Promoters of products and services might choose certain expressions, including attractive pictures of their products and services, which might easily influence the behaviour of rural consumers or users. Promotion of products and services must refer to the health hazards, if any, and be entirely transparent in order to ensure that rural customers and users also understand what they are paying for. The Code further defines 'advertising' or 'advertisement' as 'any form of marketing communication' which may be carried by the media, which incidentally has been subject to various criticisms almost all over the world for exceeding their limit.

It is common knowledge that in order to earn their additional financial benefits on their performance, marketeers, whether directly or indirectly, might be over-enthusiastic to sell their products and/or services.

The Consolidated ICC Code also developed certain General Provisions on Advertising and Marketing Communication Practice. As Basic Principles, it stated that all marketing communications should be *decent*, *honest* and *truthful* in addition to their being conformed to the regulatory limits. There is no reason why these criteria may not be applied to rural marketing. It has already been indicated that in promoting any product or services in rural areas' marketeers, particularly those who may belong to large institutions, must promote their products and services in a way which would not disturb the rural ethics and standards of decency. No attempt should be made to align them to urban tasters and the standards of decency as a mode of marketing unless the rural consumers gradually volunteer to align themselves to urban tasters and practices. Marketing in rural areas must particularly be socially responsible in nature.

Article 5 of the Code provides that marketing communications should be truthful and not misleading. Whether marketing communications are addressed to urban or rural consumers, this recommendation is fundamentally important for all forms of marketing communications. One of the ways of avoiding misleading communications is to make statements in them which are simple to understand for everybody and jargon-free. This is particularly true of communications sent to prospective customers by e-mails.[2] Communications, where translated into

---

[2]See further C Chatterjee, *E-Commerce Law for Business Managers*, London, Financial World Publishing (2002).

different languages to cater for rural customers must also ensure that they are comprehensible to them. Marketing communications particularly in relation to children's products must not be conducted in a way which might entice the parents/guardians to buy them for their children. All aspects of products, including their ingredients, should be clearly stated in the publicity materials. The issue of health and safety of consumers, including children and young people, is of paramount importance. Any element of risks or health-related issues, that is, who should not use a particular product should be clearly and truthfully stated on labels and in communications written in different local languages. In promoting products, particularly for children and young people, the issue of rural values should be borne in mind as an element of social responsibility.

The legal position of rural customers as to their rights must not be disregarded. These rights primarily relate to return of goods if not fit for the purpose, payments of compensation in the event of any health hazards or risks arising from the use of products, substitution of products, and refund of the money paid for by the consumer. The circumstances in which these privileges would be available should be clearly stated in the conditions of sale. Data of consumers may not be saved or maintained by the providers of goods and services without their consent nor should they be transmitted to affiliated business houses without their consent. Firms intending to set up their branches or subsidiaries in rural areas should train their staff and the local people to develop their businesses. The headquarters staff should be chosen very carefully who are free from prejudices and any sense of discrimination. In fact, the headquarters staff may find it very useful to interact with the local staff with a view to learning the geographic area, the local habits, purchasing capacity and their aspirations too. The local rural people are usually very eager to welcome people from urban firms and to work together, which would in reality be a learning process for both the parties.

Under the Chapter on Sales Promotion (Chapter 4), the Code identified certain principles governing sales promotion, namely (a) that all sales promotions efforts should treat all customers fairly and honourably; this latter term – honourably – is extremely important in that during a sales promotion activity, the promoters must not have any prejudice against rural customers; (b) that all sales promotion activities must make attempts to meet consumer aspirations as much as possible – this will not only make the consumers happy which eventually will create confidence in the minds of the rural communities; (c) that all obligations that may arise from sales promotion activities should be fulfilled promptly and efficiently; (d) that all participants involved in sales promotion activities must remain transparent of the terms and conduct of these activities; (e) that sales promotion activities must not aim at monopolising the market(s) – this principle is important for fulfilling the main objective of this work; if there exist a number of firms in a rural area, employment will rise; peoples' financial position would be better; savings with the help of financial institutions will also rise, which would eventually increase investments; and (f) that sales promotion activities must not have any adverse impact upon the prospective consumers and must not be carried out in a manner, which might bring sales promotion into disrepute.

Chapter C of this Code deals with Direct Marketing, but in the rural areas in Africa and Asia, in particular, direct marketing that is very much promoted through electronic media may not have much relevance to those remote rural areas in which many consumers do not have the privilege of using telephones or televisions or computers. Therefore, in the context of this work any discussion of this form of marketing may not be most appropriate. By the same token, a discussion of the contents of Chapter D – Advertising and Marketing Communications using Digital Interactive Media and those of Chapter E – Environment Claims in Marketing Communications has been omitted.

The International Chamber of Commerce has a number of Codes on Marketing Practice, namely:

- The ICC Code of Sales Promotion;
- The ICC International Code on Sponsorship;
- The ICC/ESOMAR International Code of Marketing and Social Research Practice;
- The ICC Revised Guidelines on Advertising and Marketing on the Internet;
- The ICC International Code of Direct Marketing; and
- The ICC International Code of Direct Selling

In the context of this work, there is hardly any point in going into any details of any of these Codes; the theme of this work is to establish how marketing and sales of goods and services with the involvement of the rural people may prove to be a direct factor of rural development. However, during the skills development process through training by the corporate entities concerned, they may like to introduce to the local trainees some of the important and relevant aspects of these codes of conduct. Take, for example, the ICC International Code of Environmental Advertising, 2001. The impact of environmental advertising may not be sufficiently clear to many rural people simply because the vast majority of developing countries tend to ignore the need for developing rural areas and the people therein. But, if corporate entities, whether local or foreign, are persuaded to explore the potential markets in the rural areas of a country with the participation of the local people, then, public awareness level of these people in relation to many relevant issues pertaining to marketing and sales including the impact of environmental advertising may also be raised; but during the process of imparting instructions, their lack of knowledge in regard to environmental advertising should not be exploited. In its Basic Principles, the ICC International Code of Environmental Advertising provides, inter alia, that environmental advertising should be legal, decent, honest and truthful (Article 1), and in Article 2, it states that these should not be concluded in a way which would abuse consumers' concern for the environment, or exploit their lack of knowledge in regard to the protection of the environment in general, and how certain products can interact with the environment. Instead, the marketeers and sellers may like to educate the local people whether the latter work for them or not. Thus, it is maintained that socio-economic development through marketing and sales is a phenomenon which may be successfully materialised if only the agents of it (marketeers and sellers) possess a totally progressive type of attitude whereby they themselves would be part of the materialisation process and involve the local people so that they also take a very proactive interest in the process.

Any attempt at achieving socio-economic development through marketing including sales of products and services would require the corporate entities, large or small, to act as model agents of socio-economic development and to shoulder a heavy burden to turn around rural areas to urban areas but within limits. Its objectives are manifold, but in the context of this work, they should be involved in providing capacity to the local rural people, transforming the rural areas into urban areas by developing industries, financial institutions and by contributing to infrastructural development. Business ethics has a prominent role to play in this entrepreneurial work; thus, it is imperative that corporate entities volunteering to embark upon this type of work themselves have high ethical standards, and also conform to the recommendations provided by certain international, inter-governmental and non-governmental institutions. This discussion starts with the recommendations of the International Chamber of Commerce (ICC), an extremely reputable non-governmental institution, but only the ethical aspects of marketing and sales-related recommendations have received attention here.

Recommendations adopted by the ICC – The International Chamber of Commerce is one of the most reputable non-governmental institutions in the world of business; many countries, particularly in the developed world, implement its recommendations; there is no reason why developing countries may not do so. Should these recommendations be incorporated into commercial contracts, the parties will be legally bound to accept them as legally binding provisions. These recommendations do contribute to developing and raising public awareness as to consumers' rights.[3] Irrespective of their country of registration or incorporation, corporate entities entering into rural areas may like to implement these recommendations and make the local people aware of them too, rather than imposing on them their corporate policies only. Rural people must also be made aware of their rights and duties as consumers. Against this background information, a brief analysis is given of certain of the ICC's Codes of Conduct relating to marketing and selling.

4.3.2 International Code of Advertising Practice, 1986[4]

This Code has two primary objectives: (a) it should work as an instrument of self-discipline and (b) ICC International Arbitral Tribunals to use it as a reference document.[5] It applies to all advertisements, corporate or otherwise, for any goods, services and facilities, and according to ICC, it should be read with other of its Codes of Marketing Practice, namely,

---

[3]See further C Chatterjee, *Legal Aspects of Transnational Marketing and Sales Contracts*, London, Cavendish (1996) at 37.
[4]ICC Publication No. 432B.
[5]C Chatterjee, *Legal Aspects of Transnational Marketing and Sales Contracts*, op. cit., at 38.

- Marketing Research Practice,
- Sales Promotion Practice,
- Direct Mail and Mail Order Sales Practice and
- Direct Sales Practice.

The International Code of Advertising Practice, 1986 set the standards of ethical conduct to be followed by anyone, including corporate entities, in regard to advertisements for the purpose of promoting products or services. In giving advertisements for products or services, the local sentiment, and ethical standards of the rural area concerned should not be ignored, that is why introduction of products or services to each rural area through advertisements may have to be different; words and pictures in them must be carefully chosen. Indeed, this applies to every aspect of an advertisement, namely, words, spoken or written, visual impact, music and sound effect; furthermore, publicity materials should not be published if their likely impact on the consumer would be adverse according to the ethical standards of the rural areas concerned. This Code defines a 'consumer' as an individual to whom an advertisement is addressed or who is likely to be reached by the advertisement.

Legality, decency, honesty, truthfulness and social responsibility are some of the basic principles on which this Code is based. In addition, this also developed certain guidelines in respect of advertising practice: not to play on superstition, not to provide any misleading information, not to exploit the lack of experience or knowledge of the consumer. One of the objectives of achieving socio-economic development in rural areas through marketing is to make the process of development interesting in order that rural people take interest in their development process. But the first effective step forward towards that goal would be to give them skills and knowledge which in due course would hopefully be passed on to the next generation too. From this standpoint, rural marketing entails even more responsibilities than urban marketing; furthermore, rural marketing and sales, when it may be directed to rural development, also entails giving training and skills to the local people within the parameters of their living environment.

No ICC Code has been developed to address the issue of rural marketing, in particular, but the provision of its various relevant Codes may be applied *mutatis mutandis* to rural marketing and sales too. Irrespective of whether it is urban marketing or rural marketing, the Code's recommendations that no misleading information may be given to customers as to the nature, composition, method, date of manufacture, fitness for purpose, range of use, commercial or geographical origin, etc.[6] According to the Code again, privacy of customers should be protected, and there should not take place any unjustifiable exploitation of goodwill of a trade name or trademark, and special warning should be incorporated into the label addressed to children for health and safety reasons.

In fact, it should be part of the socio-economic development process to persuade rural people to set up their own organisations in the form of local

---

[6]See further C Chatterjee, op. cit., at 39.

non-governmental organisations, which would attempt to raise the public awareness level relating to quality of products, as well as customer rights by holding seminars from time to time and distributing leaflets to the people in the geographic area concerned. Rapport should also be developed between these non-governmental bodies and the providers of consumer products and services. Gradually, the local employers will be going through the learning process as to how not to give publicity to products and services – a capacity-building process. According to Article 16 of this Code:

> No advertisement which contravenes this Code may be defended, and that no form of correction at a later date may be accepted.

This Code also contains guidelines for advertising products for children, which provide, inter alia, that advertisements addressed to children must not be confused with editorial or programme material. Advertisements meant especially for children's products must be drafted in the simplest possible language, but their purpose cannot be to entice the children into acquiring it through their parents or guardians as the case may be by making the description of the products glamorous and by using untrue words. Guideline 5 provides that[7]:

> No advertisements shall include any direct appeal to children or influence others' minds to buy an advertised product for them.

Advertisers should be held responsible for giving misleading advertisements for their products, even by indicating that price-wise the product should be within the easy reach of their parents or guardians. In other words, advertisements meant for children must not be persuasive in any way.

4.3.3 International Code of Sales Promotion, 1987[8]

The former version of this Code was published in 1973. The basic tenet on which the 1987 Code is based is that in sales promotion exercises, a fair balance must be struck between the interests of all parties concerned – producers, distributors and consumers. It has been the aspiration of ICC that the courts would use this Code, where relevant, as a reference document. One of the aims of this Code is to harmonise standards of sales promotion practice.[9]

This Code embraces all forms of distribution of products, marketing techniques to make goods and services attractive by offering additional benefits, such as, reduced price or even free offers, to give customers coupons, stamps, vouchers, samples and prizes. The following are the most important principles on which the Code is based:

---

[7]As stated earlier that the definition of a 'child' varies from society to society.
[8]ICC Publication No. 432A.
[9]See further C Chatterjee, op. cit., at 40.

- System of self-regulation should be based on ethical conduct;
- Sales promotion should be legal, decent, honest, truthful and should not violate the principle of fair competition;
- Terms of promotion should be equitable to all participants;
- Sales promotion must not provoke any violent or anti-social behaviour, and shall be in conformity with public morality and public interest; and
- Sales promotion presentations should ensure that they would not mislead those to whom they are addressed.

To summarise, some of the important essentials of the rules of sales promotion would be: integrity, non-exaggeration of any additional benefits, protection of consumers including children and young people, presentation of all materials and facts truthfully, honestly, decently and without crossing the boundaries of law; observance of the rules of competition in the relevant market and avoidance of misleading terms which might confuse/entice customers into purchase of the product, and tight control over intermediaries so as to ensure that they are not in breach of the essentials of a good promotional presentation.[10]

4.3.4 ICC International Code of Environmental Advertising

This Code was distributed by ICC in June 2001. ICC maintains that this Code has been widely accepted as it offers the platform for promoting high standards of ethics in marketing. It recognises social responsibilities in regard to commercial communications. ICC also hopes that the courts will use it as a reference document. This Code was developed for extending the area of self-discipline too. This version of the Code combines business ethics and the rules of the International Standard ISO 14021 in order to provide 'a practical tool to be used by all concerned with environmental advertising'.

This Code applies to all advertisements concerned not only with products but also other related issues, namely, packaging, distribution, use and services. The Code rightly pointed out that environmental claims can be made in any medium, e.g., product literature as well as via telephone or digital or electronic media. This Code contains 11 Basic Principles, but only those which are thought to be relevant, directly or indirectly to the theme of this work, have received a brief attention.

Principle 1 states that all environmental advertising should be legal, decent, honest and truthful. The message of this principle is very important for rural areas in that rural people, in general, particularly in developing countries, are not as informed of issues of consumer rights as the urban people.

Principle 2 has been exclusively devoted to 'honesty' according to which basically advertisements should not be couched or drafted in a manner, which might abuse consumers' concern for the environment, or they have the intention

---

[10]See further C Chatterjee, op. cit., at 41.

or objective to take advantage of the lack of possible knowledge of the rural people in environmental issues.

Principle 4 relates to truthful presentation of advertisements. In other words, words in them must be chosen in a way which would not mislead prospective consumers by exaggerating the presumed but not real advantages of products and abort the environmental aspects of them. Vague or non-specific claims of environmental benefits that may convey a wide range of meanings to consumers may only be made if they are substantiated as valid without qualifications. Claims such as 'environmentally friendly' or 'ecologically safe' should not be used as these claims can require a very high standard of proof.

According to Principle 9 of the Code, environmental signs or symbols should only be used in advertisements provided their sources are clearly indicated. Less informed consumers might easily be persuaded by the use of the claims 'environmentally friendly' or 'ecologically safe'.

4.3.5 The Draft UN Code of Conduct on Transnational Corporations, 1983

This embraced a number of issues also relevant to the issue of rural marketing in that in many cases marketing and sales promotion are operated by branches or subsidiaries of larger corporations which are located in overseas jurisdictions. Neither the headquarters companies nor its branches and subsidiaries may be familiar with the rural areas in a country; thus, there exists a risk that by virtue of their reputation and goodwill they will have a tendency to superimpose their business practice on rural areas at the cost of the local values and ethics, which is not an admirable practice, and which, in fact, is contrary to the very objective of achieving development through indigenous means and with indigenous peoples' participation conforming to the ethics and values of the society concerned.

Contributions of transnational corporations to developing economies may not be denied; on the other hand, in view of what has been stated above, their participation should be in conformity with the aspirations of the local people in rural areas, which should be part of the development policies of a developing State. Transnational corporations should be part of a development process to provide technical assistance which would also take the form of capacity building. Financial contributions might be necessary for them too, but under certain conditions.

According to the Draft UN Code of Conduct on Transnational Corporations, these corporations when they may be operating in foreign jurisdictions, they should adhere to the economic goals and development objectives, policies and priorities; they are also recommended to '... work seriously towards making a positive contribution to the achievement of such goals at the national and, as appropriate, the regional level...'[11] This provision would require each national government to develop its economic goals, development objectives, policies and priorities in an articulate fashion, which is unfortunately absent in many of the

---

[11]Paragraph 9 of the Draft Code.

developing countries, or even if they exist, they are not in many cases clearly drafted. This should be part of the screening system which is applicable to determining the suitability of transnational corporations for the development objectives of a host country.

Paragraph 12 of the Draft Code of Conduct recommends that these corporations while functioning in host countries should adhere to socio-cultural objectives, values and traditions of those countries. This Code also states that:

> ... while economic and technological development is normally accompanied by social changes, transnational corporations should/shall avoid practices, products or services which cause detrimental effect on cultural patterns and socio-cultural objectives as determined by governments.[12]

Again, it is for the inviting host country to make these provisions part of the investment contract. Secondly, this is particularly what this work also advocates in a country's efforts to achieve socio-economic development in rural areas with the assistance of transnational corporations.

In addition to recommending non-interference of transnational corporations in internal political affairs of a host State, and their abstention from corrupt practices, in Paragraphs 37–40 of the Draft Code provides that transnational corporations shall/should carry out their operations[13,14]:

> ... in particular production and marketing, in accordance with national laws, regulations, administrative practices and policies concerning consumer protection of the countries in which they operate.[15]

The Draft Code also recommended them to maintain the relevant international standards in performing their activities in host countries. This Code also provided that:

> Transnational corporations shall/should, in respect of the products and services which they produce or market or propose to produce or market in any country, supply to the competent authorities of that country on request or on a regular basis, as specified by these authorities, all relevant information concerning:

• Characteristics of these products or services which may be injurious to the health and safety of consumers including experimental uses and related aspects;

---

[12]Paragraph 12 of the Draft Code.
[13]Paragraphs 15 and 16 of the Draft Code.
[14]Paragraph 20 of the Draft Code.
[15]Paragraph 37 of the Draft Code.

• Prohibitions, restrictions, warnings and other public regulatory measures imposed in other countries on grounds of health and safety protection on these products or services.[16]

These provisions are self-explanatory. The Code further recommended that transnational corporations shall/should disclose to the public in the countries in which they operate all appropriate information, on the contents and the possible hazardous effect of the product they produce or in the host countries by means of labelling and accurate advertising.[17] This issue has also been dealt with by the ICC Codes and referred to in this work.

Like the ICC Code of Conduct, this UN Draft Code of Conduct also recommended that transnational corporations in carrying out their activities in host countries must pay their attention to their national laws and regulations, administrative practices and policies in regard to the preservation of their environment.[18] Developing host countries is therefore required to develop appropriate legislation for the preservation of their environment which may not be polluted by the private foreign investors invited into their countries, but they must also ensure that breaches of this legislation or administrative orders of their government are effectively enforced.

4.4 Conclusions

The principal purpose of writing this chapter was not to examine and analyse certain of the important Codes of Conduct published by the International Chamber of Commerce and the United Nations but to remind the large or other corporate entities of their responsibilities and duties when they may be involved in rural marketing with a view to achieving socio-economic development in those areas. It has been explained in this chapter that in carrying out marketing and selling functions in rural areas, in general, these entrepreneurs will have at least two major responsibilities to discharge: (a) to develop skills and knowledge in the rural people (capacity building) and (b) to create employment preferably by setting up their branches or subsidiaries, although during the initial stage of the venture they might experience certain difficulties, namely, the low-quality transport and distribution facilities, less advanced banking system and even in certain areas the lack of electricity. But this is where a collaborative arrangement with the governments, local and central, might be useful; indeed, public authorities have also a duty to support the programmes of these enterprises. How local finance and the extent to which it may be made available is a matter for the parties concerned to negotiate, and this issue has received attention in chapter 7 of this work. In the skills-building process, the entrepreneurs would be required to raise the level of public awareness in people in rural areas, and to inform them of their rights to

---

[16]Paragraphs 37 and 38 of the Draft Code.
[17]Paragraph 39 of the Draft Code.
[18]Paragraph 41 of the Draft Code.

consumer protection, hence the discussion of the relevant aspects of the various Codes of Conduct. On the other hand, entrepreneurs must not take advantage of the lack of knowledge in regard to the quality of goods and shall abstain from giving misleading advertisements of their products and services.

As stated earlier that in the business of developing rural marketing and sales the standards of ethics on the part of the entrepreneurs who are, in reality, engaged in what may be described as 'turning around' stagnant areas to vibrant ones will not only require creativity on their part but also develop interest in the process in the minds of the rural people concerned. Eventually, the ultimate aim may be achieved through what may be described as a 'participatory method' of achieving socio-economic development.

Furthermore, marketing and sales of products and services in rural areas will not only enrich the knowledge and experiences of the entrepreneurs but also expand their branches in the neglected areas of countries; thus, it can be a two-way benefit process. Moreover, these areas, when developed, may also supply them high-quality products which would cater for their businesses in urban areas too. However, rural marketing process must be ethics-based, bias-free, honest and transparent and also education-oriented.

Chapter 5

Sources of Finance for Rural Marketing and Development

Abstract

Briefly, sources of finance for rural development in developing countries have presented an almost insoluble problem. The Addis Ababa Action Agenda – Financing for Development, 2015 has received attention, Istanbul Declaration and Programme of Action, the Vienna Programme of Action for Landlocked Developing Countries for the Decade 2014–2024 have received attention. Some basic information on Microfinance at a rural level with special section in this chapter has been devoted to Professor Muhammad Yunus' work entitled 'Banker to the Poor'.

Keywords: The Addis Ababa Action Agenda; the Vienna Programme of Action for Landlocked Developing Countries; microfinance; rural; level

5.1 Introduction

In this chapter, an attempt is made to identify and examine the probable sources of finance for rural marketing and development. Most governments in developing countries seem to be reluctant to develop their rural areas for their own reasons, whether financial or otherwise. As stated earlier that most of the governments of developing countries share certain common characteristics: (a) they have failed to establish governments which will be run in consultation with the people (through non-governmental organisations) to encourage people to take interests in their country; (b) there does not often occur any continuity of policies, as with the change of governments policies tend to change; (c) it has become evident that there exists a high degree of reluctance to make education accessible to everybody, male or female; thus, the available human resources remain under-utilised; and (d) a reluctance to developing confidence in the minds of private foreign investors (transnational corporations) by operating a very neutral judiciary by separating it from the executive. It is hastened to add that the quality of the judges

Rural Marketing as a Tool for National Development, 67–79

Copyright © 2024 Charles Chatterjee

Published under exclusive licence by Emerald Publishing Limited

doi:10.1108/978-1-83608-064-020241006

may not be questioned but they tend to prefer a judiciary which is separable and separate from the executive, although it is submitted that not all developed countries have this form of judiciary.

Having briefly discussed the background to developing countries, which have some prospects of making finance available for small businesses in the rural areas of a country, it would be appropriate to examine the probable sources of finance for small businesses and/or ventures in the rural areas in a developing country, in general, although not all the developing countries are the same.

By a process of elimination, it may be stated that the standard commercial banks in a country are rather reluctant to lend (microfinance) to any small businesses/ventures without appropriate security, which condition would be very difficult to satisfy entrepreneurs of small businesses/ventures. Secondly, business houses in rural areas will have no *locus standi* to borrow even small amounts from international financial institutions such as the International Development Association – only their governments can be applicants for such loans; but then the type of businesses in which rural people may be capable of handling with little financial assistance need not be derived from large financial institutions, local or international. Thus, one is left with two choices: (a) microfinance and (b) financial contributions combined with capacity building from transnational corporations.

This chapter therefore examines two sources of finance: (a) microfinance and (b) finance from transnational corporations already working in the country concerned. It would be most appropriate to lay the foundations of financing for development by examining the Addis Ababa (Ethiopia) Action Agenda on Financing for Development discussed at a Conference there during 13–16 July 2015.

5.2 Addis Ababa Action Agenda – Financing for Development 13-16 July 2015, Addis Ababa

In its Action Agenda, the main theme of which was Financing for Development, issues such as domestic public resources and domestic and international private business and finance from other sources also received attention at the Conference. In setting a global framework for financing development post-2015, the Conference pointed out, inter alia, that although on the one hand, many developing countries have '... implemented policy framework that have contributed to increased mobilisation of domestic resources and higher levels of economic growth and social progress', on the other hand, many developing countries 'still face considerable challenges, and some have fallen further behind. Inequalities within many countries have increased dramatically'.[1,2] The Conference also stated that there was a need to ensure that the UN's development efforts enhance resilience in the face of all thereto.[3] The Conference further maintained that:

---

[1]op. cit., at 2, paragraph 3.
[2]Ibid in paragraph 4.
[3]Ibid in paragraph 4.

Solutions can be found, including through strengthening public policies, regulatory frameworks and finance at all levels, unlocking the transformative potential of people and the private sector, and incentivising changes in financing as well as consumption and production patterns to support sustainable development.[4]

This is precisely the principal theme of this work – to unlock the transformative potential of people – it is believed that in order to incentivise unlocked potential of people, interesting projects in rural areas, which would attract them, would be a good and profitable start for both the local people, the corporate entities and the government concerned.

In regard to African countries, least-developed countries, landlocked developing countries and small island developing States, the Conference registered its concern for these countries, and emphasised that they need enhanced global support to overcome their structural challenges. The Conference also reaffirmed the need to achieve a positive socio-economic transformation in Africa, and the need to address the diverse and specific development needs of middle-income countries, including the need for combating poverty in all of its forms, and supported the implementation of the relevant strategies and programmes of action including the Istanbul Declaration and Programme of Action, the SIDS Accelerated Modalities of Action (Samoa) Pathway and the Vienna Programme of Action for Landlocked Developing Countries for the Decade 2014–2024, and re-affirmed the importance of supporting the new development framework, 'the African Union's Agenda 2063' in addition to its 10-year Plan of Action in order to ensure a positive socio-economic transformation in Africa within the next 50 years.[5,6] It also identified the needs of the countries in conflict and post-conflict situations.

The Addis Ababa Conference clearly identified the issues that need the urgent attention of the international community, albeit in a broad fashion, and it also clearly emphasised the need for unlocking local human resources, which would in due course, enhance their capacity, and that development should be achieved through domestic and international private businesses, the latter obviously for enriching the skills and knowledge of domestic enterprises.

In regard to domestic public resources, the Conference noted that:

> ... well-functioning national and regional development banks can play in financing sustainable development particularly in credit market segments in which commercial banks are not fully engaged and where large financing gaps exist...[7]

---

[4]op. cit., at 2–3, paragraph 5.
[5]op. cit., in paragraph 8.
[6]Ibid; see also the UN General Assembly resolutions on the New Partnership for Africa's Development (NEPAS).
[7]op. cit., at 15, paragraph 33.

Furthermore, the Report of the Conference also stated that:

> Private business activity, investment and innovation are major drivers of productivity, inclusive of economic growth and job creation.[8]

The Report also confirmed that:

> Many people, especially women, still lack access to financial services, as well as financial literacy, which is a key for social inclusion.[9]

In addition to recognising the philanthropic donations towards socio-economic growth, and encouraging the regular flow of such donations, the Report also recognised that:

> ... micro, small and medium-sized enterprises, particularly those that are women-owned, often have difficulty in obtaining financing.[10]

It therefore encouraged increased lending to these enterprises, and the use of collateral substitutes, in addition to its plan to encourage both international and domestic banks to promote finance for micro-, small- and medium-sized enterprises through the creation of credit lines targeting these enterprises.[11] The need for an increased capacity building and technical assistance from various financial institutions was also emphasised by it.

What are needed in fact, development-oriented capital funds, preferably with public partners, blended finance, and innovative debt funding structures with appropriate risk management and regulatory frameworks, as well as capacity building in these areas.[12] The Report also recognised that foreign investors play a significant role in some developing countries' capital markets – this is a critically important issue as strong capital markets are so essential for the purpose of 'heating up' economies. The Report further stated, inter alia, that:

> Government policies can strengthen positive spill overs from foreign direct investment, such as know-how and technology, including through establishing linkages with domestic suppliers, as well as encouraging the integration of local enterprises, in

---

[8]op. cit., at 17, paragraph 35.
[9]op. cit., at 19, paragraph 39.
[10]op. cit., at 21, paragraph 43.
[11]op. cit., at 21, paragraph 43.
[12]op. cit., at 22, paragraph 43.

particular, micro, small and medium-sized enterprises in developing countries, into regional and global value chains.[13]

The Report rightly pointed out that private foreign investors may be agents for diversification of the economies of the developing, least-developed and landlocked countries, and that they should be encouraged to increase their investments in these countries by taking out risk insurance policies from the Multilateral Investment Guarantee Agency (MIGA).[14] It also recommended 'blended finance investments', including public–private partnerships, which it believes would '... serve to lower investment specific risks and incentivise additional private sector finance across key development sectors led by regional, national and subnational government policies and priorities for sustainable development.'[15]

Of course, the Report contains other very interesting recommendations on development finance, a discussion of which would be somewhat beyond the remit of this work. However, it is worth noting that the theme of this work is in line with the recommendations of the Addis Ababa Action Agenda.[16]

5.3 Some Basic Information on Microfinance

Microfinance became a popular method of financing small and medium (size) enterprises (SMEs), particularly since the 1990s, but over the last 30 years or so, this industry has grown enormously culminating in a much talked-about industry in the world of finance. There has occurred a particular shift from 'microcredit' to 'microfinance'. A growing public awareness for providing financial help to SMEs has become manifest, in consequence of which the burden of risks of lending on large banks seem to have been lessened. Microfinance is now regarded as a major source of financial services to SMEs which are no longer required to depend on a single class of financial services providers, which, of course, did not effectively provide all the financial products that poor people need to develop their businesses.[17] Furthermore, different products bear different risks, which were not favoured by SMEs.

Policy-makers are now paying attention to the new dimension to microfinance and even thinking of 'financial inclusion' in their economic plans so that access to financial services improves the ability of consumers to access markets which, in turn, would as its consequential effect contribute to economic growth and economic stability, when combined with appropriate governmental policies. The issues of consumer protection and financial capability of markets have also

---

[13]op. cit., at 22, paragraph 45.

[14]op. cit., at 23, paragraphs 45 and 46; see also S K Chatterjee, 'The Convention Establishing the Multilateral Investment Guarantee Agency', op. cit.

[15]op. cit., at 25, paragraph 48.

[16]A critical analysis of the Agenda was also published by the Addis Ababa Civil Society Forum on Financing for Development on 22 July 2015.

[17]See further T Ehrbeck, M. Pickens and M. Tarazi, 'Financially Inclusive Ecosystems: The Roles of Government Today', Focus Note 76, CGAP, Washington, DC (2012 – February).

become a popular phenomenon not only in the developed world but also across its shores. SMEs, on the other hand, are now required to be more organised and productive for becoming eligible for microfinance which will directly contribute to the progress of rural development.

One of the significant developments that has taken place in regard to micro-finance is that it is no longer in the exclusive domain of donors alone; micro-finance investment vehicles make funds available to private and quasi-private sectors too. Donors have now taken the role of facilitators which allows them to support the development of projects by providing information and financial advice that would contribute to the growth and establishment of financial infra-structures, which is precisely what rural areas need, rather than adhering to their traditional role of providers of funds for loan capital and offering subsidies to SMEs.

Despite the growing performance of microfinance, it is important to identify some of its limitations:

- As stated earlier that in order to operate any form of regulated finance, peoples' banking awareness and traditional habits of keeping money at home should be urgently changed; but the caution must be entered that their advanced knowledge in banking must be directed at the advantage of regulatory mea-sures in keeping banking system healthy and as risk-free as possible, rather than opening doors to abuse of these measures.[18] This point is important to bear in mind as countries such as Kenya and Malawi are already engaged in pro-moting mobile money, and even the development of branchless banking, which would eventually be invited by rural markets almost everywhere in the world.[19]
- Microfinancing system has already been subject to criticism on the grounds that its success may not be guaranteed. Microfinance operations have often been subsidised, particularly in those of the countries in which per capita income is extremely low.[20] Furthermore, only flow of finance to an enterprise might not lead to its success; capacity building, technical assistance, product development knowledge must also be developed as otherwise, microfinance operations have to subsidise SMEs for an indefinite period of time.

---

[18] A Chaia, A Dalal, T Goland, M J Gonzalez, J Morduch and R Schiff, 'Half the World Is Unbanked', *Financial Access Initiative Framing Note* (2009), New York, Financial Access Initiative.

[19] See further C Alexandre, 'Policymakers Create Room for Experiments with Banking Beyond Branches', Global Savings Forum, Bill and Melinda Gates Foundation, Seattle, Washington (2010); see also S Johnson and S Arnold, 'Financial Exclusion in Kenya: Examining the Changing Picture 2006–2009 in Financial Inclusion in Kenya', Survey Results and Analysis from FinAccess, 2009 (S Arnold et al.) Chapter 5, Nairobi FSD Kenya and Central Bank of Kenya (2011).

[20] See further S Wiesner and D Quinn, 'Can "Bad" Microfinance Practices be the Consequence of too much Funding Chasing too Few Microfinance Institutions?' Discussion Paper 1, No. 2 ADA, Luxembourg (2010).

- Furthermore, Randomized Controlled Trials (RCTs) found that there does not always exist any correlation between increases in consumption and poverty reduction – it is still believed that without any predictable reasonable income, consumption level may not increase. In order for microfinancing to be successful, the market behaviour, and the understanding of how the poor need and use financial services should be carefully studied prior to being involved in this kind of financing. Johnson and Arnold also maintained that persistent barriers to inclusion of microfinance to a financial system is also another important factor for its mixed success.[21,22]
- In microfinance, costs are high, and the sources of revenue are not remarkably predictable. This is primarily owing to the fact that rural people have limited investment opportunities as well; furthermore, urban banks usually lack the knowledge as to how to expand rural markets. This situation is further aggravated by the rural habit of borrowing money from relatives, rather than finance houses, in consequence of which the risk of absence of high flow of microfinance exists. Thus, in order to make microfinance a profitable source of income for lenders, a considerable amount of background work for rural markets would be essential.

These observations on the efficacy or inefficacy of microfinancing system should not deter one from developing the microfinance system in rural areas of developing countries provided of course, as stated earlier, that the attitudes of rural people towards finance from external institutions have gradually changed, in addition to involving the rural people in actual industries which should provide them incentives to take advantage of microfinance, and if that should happen, the world of microfinance might also change their strategies for lending too.[23]

5.4 Microfinance at a Rural Level

In his book entitled Banker to the Poor: The Story of the Grameen Bank, Professor Muhammad Yunus, who was awarded Nobel Peace Prize in 2006, very clearly explained the kind of hurdles he was required to cross over to fulfil his ambition of setting up a Grameen bank (a bank for village people) in order to enable them to get out of their poverty-stricken lives. His commitment to eradicating poverty was unquestionable for he stated that:

> Poverty is a disease which has a paralysing effect on mind and body.[24]

---

[21]K O'Dell, 'Measuring the Impact of Microfinance: Taking Another Look', Grameen Foundation, Washington, DC (2010).

[22]op. cit., (2011).

[23]For detailed discussion of microfinance, see J Ledgerwood, *Microfinance Handbook: An Institutional and Financial Perspective*, Washington, DC, World Bank (Latest edition), first published in 1998.

[24]M Yunus, *Banker to the Poor: The Story of the Grameen Bank*, London, Aurum Press Ltd (1998) at 82.

According to the author:

> In 1996, James D Wolfensohn, President of the World Bank, acknowledged: "micro-credit programmes have brought the vibrancy of the market economy to the poorest villages and people of the world. This business approach to the alleviation of poverty has allowed millions of individuals to work their way out of poverty with dignity.[25]

Microfinance system had to go through a long teething problem owing to the perception in the banking world that without a guarantee (which operates as a security against a bank loan) no bank loan may be allowed. The importance of guarantees in the case of large loans may not be denied, but bank loans of small amounts for rural development may be described as loans *sui generis*.

Attempts at socio-economic development, through development aid by international institutions have, in general, failed for a variety of reasons. Yunus, in his Chapters respectively 2 and 9 entitled 'The World Bank, Washington DC November 1993' and 'Banking: Climbing the Prison Walls of Collateral, 1976' clearly identified the failures of achieving socio-economic development through aid and the obstacles even to small amounts of loans from banks against collaterals, the sole purpose of which is to allow poor people to become financially self-sufficient and to develop some skills in themselves.

The primary theme of this work is also that developing countries, in general, may not any longer depend on the generosity of their governments for a variety of reasons, a discussion of which would be beyond the remit of this work. However, this work maintains that unless a country develops her rural areas, particularly with the participation of the local people, which would also in the process develops human resources in addition to a democratic form of government recognising the basic rights and freedoms of their people, socio-economic development of these countries would remain a far cry.

This work therefore chose marketing as an agent of development in rural areas which would be financially viable provided a microfinance system is made available for the purpose; also provided that corporate entities provide them training which would develop the rural people's skills and knowledge in their chosen industries; also provided that some finance is also made available to them by those corporate entities which may be recovered by them in due course after the production phase has commenced.

The contribution of development aid should not be denied altogether, provided of course, it is combined with capacity building. Hence the other idea of development would be to invite private foreign entities (usually known as transnational corporations) on BOT (Build, Operate and Transfer) basis, which would automatically entail capacity building for the local people, particularly, people in the rural areas of a country. This process will require the foreign entity to buy-back

---

[25]M Yunus, op. cit., at 25.

the high-quality products for its own domestic market as well as foreign markets which would eventually be served by the host country concerned. Thus, the rural areas should take interests in such endeavours and would reap the financial benefits combined with skills and knowledge – a direct means of utilising the unused human resources in a country.

No loan is risk-free. Despite instances of non-repayment of loans on microfinance basis, its success story has been provided by Professor Yunus in Chapter 24 entitled 'International Replications' in his work. By the time his work was published in 1998, he recorded replication of Grameen-type credit programmes in 59 countries, not only in developing countries but also in some of the developed countries.

In Africa, 22 countries →   Burkina Faso, the Central African Republic, Chad, Egypt, Ethiopia, Ghana, Kenya, Lesotho, Mali, Malawi, Mauritania, Morocco, Nigeria, Sierra Leone, Somalia, South Africa, Sudan (North), Tanzania, Togo, Uganda, Zanzibar and Zimbabwe.

In Asia, 16 countries →   Afghanistan, Bangladesh, Bhutan, Cambodia, China, Fiji, India, Indonesia, Kyrgyzstan, Lebanon, Malaysia, Nepal, Pakistan, the Philippines, Sri Lanka and Vietnam.

In Australasia, 1 country →   Papua New Guinea.

In the Americas, 15 countries →   Argentina, Bolivia, Brazil, Canada, Chile, Colombia, Dominican Republic, Ecuador, El Salvador, Guatemala, Guyana, Jamaica, Mexico, Peru and the US.

In Europe, 5 countries →   Albania, France, the Netherlands, Norway and Poland.[26]

There is no doubt that microfinance is now an established form of finance, which may be utilised by small industries or any other ventures, which may be developed with relatively small funds. As stated earlier, no loan is risk-free; but even though microfinance is allowed without any security, one should look into the rate of failures, in percentage terms, in making re-payment of loans. Incidentally, it may be worth mentioning that lenders may like to supervise the progress of industries or ventures to which loans have been allowed. Traditional commercial banks are now required to change their views on lending money on a microfinance basis. Given the merits of developing industries and other ventures with the privilege of ownership by the local rural people, this form of financing should be regarded as an agent of socio-economic development.

---

[26]This information has been copied from the book authored by Professor M Yunus, op. cit., at 182, and they cover the period until 1998, that is, the date on which his work was first published.

Development aid from international financial institutions has remained with us for a very long time, but its contribution towards socio-economic development of countries should be critically examined. The borrowers (the States Members of these institutions) will be required to re-pay the large, borrowed amounts with interest thereon over a period of time. If development aid fails to develop an economy, the recipient will still be required to pay back the loan. It is a burden on the borrowing State concerned. Microfinance, in contrast, does not entail any large amount of borrowing; it does not require the borrower concerned to remain finance-dependant. It is in the interest of the borrower entrepreneur that it should re-pay the loan as soon as possible; thus, there exists a genuine interest to develop the business profitably as soon as possible. Furthermore, it has the other positive dimension – the industry or venture, as the case may be, will provide skills and knowledge and of course increase employment. Should commercial banks wish to participate in this sort of lending they will be required to go above their prejudice, if any, against microfinance without the support of securities.

5.5 An Evaluation of Microfinance

In their report of June 2015 entitled *The Political Economy of Microfinance: Financialising Poverty*, the World Bank depicted a rather mixed picture of microfinance. This report stated, inter alia, that[27]:

> Fifteen years on, the microfinance industry is estimated at $60-100 billion, with 200 million clients, but the results have been mixed. Critics cite modest benefits associated with microcredit, over indebtedness, and a trend toward commercialization that is less focused on serving the poor.[28]

This report also maintained that although the initial narrative around microfinance was expected to unleash the entrepreneurial spirit of the poor which would lead to a significant growth and poverty reduction, it was never, in reality, a viable expectation.[29]

This statement leads one to identify the reasons for microfinance being a not-so-successful programme after all. There may be several reasons for microfinance's mixed progress: (a) do the recipients have the appropriate knowledge and training in dealing in microfinance? (b) are the economies and societies in the developing world, in general, psychologically prepared to utilise this source of finance? (c) the issue of costs in obtaining and managing it; and (d) do the rural people, in general, have sufficient knowledge and training in entrepreneurship? Was the microfinance system conceived merely as a lofty idea by some without

---

[27]The other title of this publication is *Does Microfinance Still Hold Promise for Reaching the Poor*, 30 March 2015.

[28]op. cit., at 2.

[29]Ibid.

making an appropriate empirical study? It has been pointed out in this work that the matrix of rural development is very different from that of urban development; and this is a fundamentally important issue in that in most countries (other than countries such as Singapore) villages outnumber urban areas. Anybody engaged in development work should bear these issues in mind, more particularly that 'one size does not fit all'. It is also important to identify the extent of human and natural resources in addition to the lack of education, infrastructure and communication system. Furthermore, the majority of people in any part of the world find it difficult to understand finance and financial institutions. These are some of the primary reasons why this work promotes training of people for skills development through industries.

The contribution of microfinance to development process in developing countries was examined by R Cull, then the lead Economist in the Finance and Private Sector Development Team of the World Bank's Development Research Group, and he maintained, inter alia, that one may not see anything 'transformational in terms of household incomes, wealth or poverty levels'.[30] According to him, under the microfinance system, lending incur higher costs in making smaller loans in consequence of which borrowers are charged higher interest rates; but his rather pessimistic view on the current microfinance system became evident when he stated that:

> The notion that we can serve the poorest of the poor [using microfinance] without reliance on subsidy is far-fetched at this point. We will need to make changes not only to the model but to the delivery mechanism.[31]

Cull's findings were based on six experimental studies he carried out on microcredit ranging from Ethiopia to Morocco to Mexico. He also observed that different types of microfinance institutions cater for different market segments, with NGOs and non-bank financial institutions targeting the poorest. Having drawn on data from the Microfinance Information Exchange (MIX) and the International Finance Corporation (IFC) that spanned for a period of 2006–2012, Cull traced the growth and development of these models from low profitability to growth and increases in the number of branches; according to him, young African microfinance institutions performed very well. He further stated that Greenfields were an effective way to reach a large number of people, and that they seemed to be commercially viable and sustainable; unfortunately, they were 'not reaching the poorest of the poor'.[32] The report went on to state that very few microfinance institutions were found to be profitable; furthermore, according to Cull, subsidy per borrower was much higher for borrowers at the higher end of the loan scale; in other words, subsidies were not pro-poor.[33] Cull therefore suggested a variety of

---

[30]op. cit., at 2.
[31]Ibid.
[32]Ibid.
[33]Ibid.

measures to improve on the current microfinancing system in the hope that it would benefit the poorest of the poor. He highlighted measures such as technological innovations, mobile banking services, a better understanding of client needs including savings devices, electronic payments and more flexible loan re-payment schedules.

According to Mr Sebastian A Molineus, Director of the Word Bank Group Finance and Markets Global Practice, 'there is no one size fits all answer to microfinance;' there also exist a large range of providers that are needed for full financial inclusion, namely, banks and non-bank financial institutions, NGOs, etc. In other words, a multi-tiered approach would be necessary; and that the entire industry should be subject to the appropriate legislation, regulations and supervision.[34,35]

In its Report of 2017, the International Finance Corporation (IFC), on the other hand, provided a rather encouraging view on microfinance, which, according to it, has built a good track record as a critical tool in the fight against poverty. Over the past 15 years, it has reached approximately 130 million clients, but unfortunately, microfinance still reaches only 20% of its potential market. Nearly, 3 billion people in the developing world have little or no access to formal financial services. As stated earlier, the larger part of a country usually consists of rural areas where there are more people; finance should be made available to them to allow them to attain economic stability through their own enterprises, which the usual sources of finance are unable to do in the contemporary world of finance. Private microfinance may have a significant development impact and improve people's lives.

Since the 1990s IFC has led innovation in microfinance whereby technology has been developed to develop skills in people '... policy to help financial institutions reach a greater number of people in a more cost-effective way.'[36] In achieving its goal, IFC effectively combines investment and advisory services to a range of financial intermediaries. By 2014, IFC, through its Global Credit Bureau Programme created or significantly improved credit bureaus in more than 30 countries.

In his work entitled 'The World Bank and Microfinance: An elephant trying to build a bird nest,' David Puglielli observed that, governments and international organisations are only recently realising the advantages of providing microenterprise with credit. Financial institutions have been created to alleviate the financial repression of small industries such as Grameen Bank of Bangladesh, but the major leaders of microenterprises are informal credit institutions. He further observed that the problem of knowledge is the primary constraint of the World Bank's microlending potential.[37] This work therefore placed emphasis on the development of skills of people, including women, living in deep rural areas in developing countries.

---

[34]Ibid.
[35]See further the World Bank's Financial Inclusion Support Framework (FISF).
[36]op. cit.
[37]P. 6.

5.6 Conclusions

In his work, Professor Yunus aptly stated that:

> It's not people who aren't credit-worthy; its banks that aren't people-worthy.[38]

This statement is very insightful. Financial institutions often disregard the potentials of people who are their real customers; however, over the recent past, particularly in the developed world, financial institutions seem to be more interested in institutional investors than ordinary customers as the former provide them more profits than the latter. But financial institutions should also take interest in rural development, as eventually, there will hardly be much differences between developed rural areas with industries, educational institutions, medical facilities, etc. and the developed urban areas. In other words, they should be agents of developments too.

Developing countries have remained so for a very long time, indeed. It is basically a man-made misery, which can be eradicated by human beings. Often, small arrangements are more successful than big ones. Human beings have their fundamental right to live and learn the way they wish, as long as it is in a lawful way. They must be emancipated from poverty and prejudices against them.

---

[38]https://ia801303.us.archive.org/20/items/BankerToThePoor/yunus.pdf

Chapter 6

Whether Socio-Economic Development May Be Achieved Through Rural Marketing

Abstract

This chapter has briefly discussed the problems of defining development and underdevelopment, and Gustavo Esteva's opinion that 'underdevelopment' was invented. The Proposal for Action of the First UN Development Decade (1960–70), Mr Robert S McNamara's view (President of the World Bank in the 1970s) on development, the Western World's Perception of Development, the |Nature of the UN Institution for Socio-Economic Development in Developing Countries, the role of International Trade and Development have been discussed in this chapter.

Keywords: Underdevelopment; invented; First UN Development Decade; Mr Robert McNamara's view on development; the UN Institute for Socio-economic Development

6.1 Introduction

Over the past few decades, the idea of 'development' has perhaps been subject to most interpretations in social sciences and in particular, Economics. But nobody has defined the term; the best that has been done so far is to describe it. According to the Concise Oxford Dictionary, 'Development' would mean 'a stage of growth or advancement'.[1] One has to consider what does 'growth and advancement' stand for? The former colonies, soon after they attained their independence from their colonial masters, they aspired to experience 'growth' and 'advancement', which has already been proved to be wrong.

---

[1] Oxford, Clarendon Press (1990) at 319.

Rural Marketing as a Tool for National Development, 81–99
Copyright © 2024 Charles Chatterjee
Published under exclusive licence by Emerald Publishing Limited
doi:10.1108/978-1-83608-064-020241007

The term 'underdeveloped' was coined by the US President, Harry Truman, in 1949 when he declared in his inauguration speech the Southern hemisphere as 'underdeveloped areas'.[2] From a psychological standpoint, this new expression had two dimensions:

(1) the US's economic strength at the material time made Truman launch the idea of development without a precise meaning attached to it, and it prompted the United States and other rich States to provide aid to the newly de-colonised States, without embarking upon any thorough research whether financial aid alone would develop the 'underdeveloped' countries or whether it would be another phase of colonisation – financial colonisation. Of course, the United States was then determined to thwart the march of the Soviet Union, which by the 1950s became a rich and industrialised economy without pursuing capitalism. The US Aid Plan of 1960 simply bolstered further the US position in the so-called development programmes.

(2) the second psychological factor that contributed to the aid-giving process was the aspiration of the former colonies to pursue Westernisation in their parts of the world too, but sadly, their aspiration was never materialised unless one cites rather odd examples such as India.[3,4]

Sachs rightly pointed out that '... development is much more than just a socio-economic endeavour'.[5] Westernisation allured the former colonies without any realisation on their part that socio-economic development is a process which entails a successful completion of a number of its essentials, which have received attention in a separate location of this chapter.

According to Gustavo Esteva, the word 'underdevelopment' was invented.[6] Indeed, the United Nations categorises countries in the following way: developed, developing and least developed. However, the 'concept of underdevelopment' is usually associated with President Truman. In his speech on 20 January 1949, that is, the day on which he took office, he said, inter alia, that:

> The old imperialism – exploitation for foreign profit – has no place in our plans. What we envisage is a programme of development based on the concepts of fair dealing.[7]

---

[2] See W Sachs, Introduction to the Work entitled, *The Development Dictionary: A Guide to Knowledge and Power*, Johannesburg, Witwatersrand University Press (also Zed Books Ltd London & New York) 2001, at 2; See also *Documents on American Foreign Relations*, Connecticut, Princeton University Press (1967).

[3] See further W Sachs, op. cit., at 4.

[4] China is not included in this group of countries, as she was never colonised by any Power.

[5] W Sachs, op. cit., at 1.

[6] Gustavo Esteva, 'Development' in W Sachs (ed), *The Development Dictionary: A Guide to Knowledge as Power*, Johannesburg, Witwatersrand University and Zed Books Ltd, London (2001) at 6.

[7] *Documents on American Foreign Relations*, op. cit.

But Truman's aspirations have not materialised as yet; on the contrary, 'economically backward areas' have gone, in general, even more backward. These are two basic reasons for this failure: (a) internal and (b) external. Whereas internal factors basically relate to (i) the nature of the governance in power; (ii) very little or no emphasis given on the promotion or enrichment of human resources; (iii) undue emphasis on private foreign investments; (iv) almost no programme for rural (remote parts of the country) development; (v) no reliable infrastructure; and (vi) the lack of sufficient emphasis on small and cottage industries and improvement of the banking system among others; the external factors would include dependence on foreign aid from various Western States and international organisations and the dream of Westernisation rather than developing the country through indigenous means.

De-colonisation was good, but the vast majority of the newly-born countries jumped from the 'frying pan' into the 'fire' so to say. They have effectively intensified their financial dependence on others – another form of colonisation, and in these circumstances political independence of the colonies proved to be meaningless, for political independence without a reasonable degree of financial independence is meaningless. It is submitted that attainment of financial and economic independence entails a long-drawn process, but for the reasons stated above, the vast majority of the newly-born States have failed to tread this path.

Colonisation of countries, which, if one seriously considers human psychology of domination by one over others, was inevitable, but 'colonisation of minds' proved to have direct effect on the colonised people. They seem to have lost their confidence in themselves; and volunteered to be subject to another form of colonisation – 'Westernisation' of their societies and countries.

In the meantime, invention of words and phrases such as 'underdevelopment' or 'economically backward areas' or 'the dark continents', which was further fuelled by prejudices against the colonised people, simply developed inferiority complex among the general public culminating in the lack of self-confidence. This is not to entirely blame the rich Western world, but to simply state the historical facts; of course, the former colonised people also should have turned their wheels against Westernisation; its glamour had a mesmerising effect on them. They went for an easy option, which back-fired on them.

Gustavo Esteva rightly pointed out that:

> Today, for two-thirds of the people of the world, underdevelopment is a threat that has already been carried out; . . . it impedes thinking of one's own objectives, as Nyerere wanted; it undermines confidence in oneself and one's own culture. . .[8]

'Development' stands for a process through which the potentials of an object or even human beings are released. Development leads to enrichment of human knowledge and skills, which, in turn, leads to growth, which in turn, leads to further growth. It also leads to a gradual process of social change (*Entwicklung –*

---

[8]Gustavo Esteva, op. cit., at 7–8.

Justus Moser, conservative founder of social history).[9] The term 'Development' seems to have developed a new connotation since the days of de-colonisation of the former colonies; it stood mainly for materialism; the emphasis was not laid on bringing out the potentials of countries and peoples therein. Private foreign investors crowded the newly-found markets, which was very alluring to the local, newly-independent people who were attracted to materialism.

The United States was never a formal colonial power, but the Truman Declaration of 1949 seems to have prompted both the US government and the US business houses to spread their net of wealth almost everywhere, particularly, in the former colonised areas. Almost everybody in those areas found Americanism attractive and worth following. The US Aid programmes, including the Point Four Programmes, convinced the former colonised people what would be the objectives of 'development'. They construed it mostly in terms of material possession, did not want to achieve development through a process (*Entwicklung*). The irony of it became soon evident. American products soon became available on the markets of former colonies.

The UN objectives of 'development', on the other hand, was ambitious and realistic. 'Development' at least during its early days was predominantly concerned with 'economic development' as if the societal dimension to it was not needed. The correct expression would be 'socio-economic development'. Indeed, in 1962, the Economic and Social Council of the United Nations (ECOSOC) recommended the integration of both the dimensions to 'development'. The Proposals for Action of the First UN Development Decade (1960–70) stated that:

> The problem of the underdeveloped countries is not just growth, but development... Development is growth and change. Change, in turn, is social and cultural as well as economic, and qualitative as well as quantitative... The key concept must improve quality of peoples' life.[10]

Improved quality of peoples' life is one of the key objectives of socio-economic development; this would entail health, education, capacity building for knowledge, skills and employability particularly in the rural areas of a country which does not necessarily require to increase foreign debts; local entrepreneurs jointly can also provide funds to small to medium industries, and in particular, to the agricultural sector of an economy.

Walter Rostow was also equally concerned with social aspects of development, rather than solely economic growth which may be quantifiable.[11] Paul Baran also

---

[9]W Arthur Lewis, *The Theory of Economic* Growth, Homewood, Illinois, Richard D Irwin (1955).

[10]UN, *The UN Development Decade: Proposals for Action*, New York, UN (1962).

[11]Walter W Rostow, *The Stages of Economic Growth: A Non-Communist Manifesto*, Cambridge, Cambridge University Press (1960).

maintained that economic development implied a thorough transformation of the economic, social and political structures of the society.[12]

The UN Research Institute for Social Development (UNRISD) was established in 1963 in recognition of the inter-connection/interdependence of social and economic factors and the need for harmonising socio-economic planning.[13] Sadly, UNRISD's sustainable ideas failed owing to increasing inequalities within societies.

Until 1970, the Western World visualised 'development' through the eyes of higher GNP. It was in 1970 that Robert S McNamara, then President of the World Bank (IBRD) who recognised that high rate of growth was not a necessary indicator of socio-economic development.[14] Whereas the First Development Decade considered the social aspect and economic aspect separately for development rather than taking an integrated approach, the Second Development Decade merged the two. On 24 October 1970, the International Development Strategy called for a global strategy embracing all aspects of socio-economic development – a unified approach was adopted for development. The following were embraced into this approach:

- To include people from all sectors for change and development;
- To achieve structural change which would contribute to the national development process and that this process must be participatory;
- To aim social equity, including the achievement of an equitable distribution of income and wealth within a State; and
- To accord priority to the development of human resources and to meet the needs of children.[15]

6.2 The Western World's Perception of 'Development'

- The Western World upon which the developing countries primarily depended for achieving their mission lacked a clear idea and policy as to how to break the grounds for it. They tested and tried various methods to achieve the missions of the newly-independent States, but only to meet with failure. In sum, developed countries, in general, were not themselves required to go through this process, which should not be compared with the reconstruction of the French and German economies after the Second World War.

---

[12]Paul N Baran, *The Political Economy of Growth*, New York, Monthly Review Press (1957).

[13]One of UNRISD's best published works is entitled, *The Quest for a Unified Approach to Development*, Geneva (1980); see also *An Approach to Development Research*, Geneva (1979).

[14]Robert S McNamara, 'The True Dimension of the Task', 1 *International Development Review* (1970).

[15]See UNRISD, *The Quest for a Unified Approach to Development* (1950) op. cit.; see also G Esteva, op. cit., at 14.

- Only financial aid cannot usher a development process but giving of aid to developing countries from all sources became a common phenomenon, which unfortunately still exists. As explained earlier that this process has simply over-burdened developing countries with debts; in other words, their political independence has created 'debt dependence' for them.
- Until about the 1980s, the general belief of the 'developers' was that in view of the economic backwardness of the developing countries, they should operate what is known as 'inward-looking strategy', whereas developed countries by virtue of their developed economies should adopt and operate an 'outward-looking strategy'. They failed to see the inter-relationship between the two strategies.
- Developing countries, on the other hand, in general, aspired 'Westernisation' as a 'quick-fix' for their socio-economic development, without realising that development must be achieved by themselves through indigenous means; the developers should be there primarily for capacity building.
- The advent of private foreign investors (transnational corporations) had produced a mesmerising effect on developing countries, in general, as they also created employment for them, albeit often in small numbers; in contracting, developing countries generally surrendered themselves to the private foreign investors, by not providing for restrictions as to their operation and also by not providing for capacity building, buy-back, etc. provisions, at least during the initial period.
- Developing countries are required to develop their 'screening policies' and also at the same time assure private foreign investors of their protection of investments under public international law. In other words, bi-lateral investment treaties should be urgently reviewed to strike a balance between the interests of developing host States and private foreign investors.
- Peace is a condition to progressing with developmental activities. Peace at both national and international levels has been conspicuously absent particularly since the destruction of the World Trade Centre in New York in 2001. Then came the new policies of disturbing current regimes, namely, those in Iraq, Syria, Yemen to name but a few, which among others gave rise to a new flow of emigration and migration of displaced individuals causing immeasurable miseries to innumerable people from different parts of the world. Nothing can be worse than making regimes unstable. Thus, the development process in many countries has come to a halt.

6.3 What Should a Developing Country Do About Her Own Socio-Economic Development?

Based on what has been discussed above, it may be concluded that socio-economic development is a country-specific affair. 'One size fits all' formula will not do. Like human bodies, each country's geography, political structure, human and natural resources are different; furthermore, the capacity to absorb development and to maintain it at a desired level will vary from country to country. It is confirmed that there is a need for finance to achieve development and to maintain it at a desired level will vary from country to country. It is also confirmed that there is a need for finance to achieve development; however, too much of borrowed finance simply creates 'dependency' on the lenders.

The initial problem with 'development' is that there does not exist any precise definition of the term. As stated earlier that the so-called 'development' has 'tried' and 'tested' various methods of developing countries' economies, but not much has been achieved. But of course, they should not share the entire blame for it themselves; many regimes in the world have failed to recognise that 'development' of a country is a matter of 'fundamental right' which should be allowed to be enjoyed and utilised by their people. A clear recognition of this 'right' by the regimes would have provided impetus to the general population in the country concerned to take the initiative to develop their economies and also human potentials.

However, various authors have attempted to define the term 'development' according to their own understanding of it. Whereas Niall MacDermot believes that in its international dimension,

> ... the right to development implies the rule of peace, the existence of a satisfactory environment and the introduction of a more just economic order, so that each people, each individual, profits from the common heritage of mankind and the efforts of all strata of society are justly rewarded.[16]

Luis Pásara emphasised the difficulties in giving any articulate definition of 'development'; he believed that 'development' is unavoidably a political issue.[17] Perhaps Luis Pásara meant to say that it is closely connected to the political policies of the country concerned. This is where the problem really arises. If a government is undemocratic, with its attendant adverse consequences, then development will be subject to its perception of it, and this statement may be verified by referring to the regimes in many of the developing countries. Rights and freedoms of peoples, opportunities for human resources development (capacity building) education, infrastructural development, including health, welfare and education are the most important essentials of 'development'. The initiatives should ideally come from the peoples, but in most cases, they are not allowed to do so. That is the unfortunate reality. In the circumstances socio-economic development of countries remains a far cry. 'Democracy' and 'Socio-Economic Development' are interwoven, although one might raise the controversy that there does not exist any precise definition of democracy either. However, without taking a too academic approach to it, it may be stated that for

---

[16] N MacDermot, Speech delivered at the Conference on Development, Human Rights and the Rule of Law, The Hague, The Report (1981) at 27–28; see also S K Chatterjee, 'International Law of Development' published in the *Encyclopaedia of Public International Law*, Max Planck Institute, vol 9, at 198–202.

[17] *Report of the Hague Conference* (1981) at 181–183.

socio-economic development purposes, freedom and rights of people are essentials of 'democracy' whereby indigenous people can take initiatives in their own development process. Indeed, if rights and freedoms are denied to a country's peoples, the government of that country must remain vulnerable.

Developing countries should in conjunction with their neighbouring countries, unless they are historically enemy countries, prevent external interventions in resolving their domestic problems, particularly, through negotiations, bearing in mind that if negotiations fail, nothing remains. Thus, it is essential that diplomats, be they represent developed or developing countries, must have mastery over negotiating techniques in resolving both internal and external differences between countries.[18]

6.4 The Nature of the UN Initiative for Socio-Economic Development in Developing Countries

The efforts of the UN in developing framework and binding resolutions on socio-economic development in developing countries are laudable. Some of the most important ones are mentioned below:

- The UN Charter, 1945;
- The Universal Declaration of Human Rights, 1948;
- The UN General Assembly Resolution entitled Permanent Sovereignty over Natural Resources, 1962 (a binding resolution developing customary norm in relation to taking of foreign assets by host States and their duty to pay appropriate compensation);
- The International Covenant on Economic, Social and Cultural Rights, 1964;
- The International Covenant on Civil and Political Rights, 1964;
- The Charter of Economic Rights and Duties of States, 1974;
- The New International Economic Order, 1974 (Res 3201 (S-VI) and 3202 (S-VI));
- Then, of course, the UN Development Decades which started in 1961;
- The Rio Declaration, 1992;
- The Addis Ababa Action Agenda on Financing for Development, 2015 which was endorsed by the UN General Assembly in its resolution 69/313 of 27 July 2015; and
- Of course, the Millennium Development Goals and Targets for 2015.

Each of these resolutions/documents/initiatives had its own objectives, but when combined them together, they give the reader a very comprehensive account of what is required for socio-economic development. Take, for example, the Addis Ababa Action Agenda, 2015. Although this Agenda was exclusively on

---

[18]See further C Chatterjee, *Negotiating Techniques in Diplomacy and Business Contracts,* Palgrave Macmillan, 2021.

Financing for Development, in Chapter II of its Report identified certain action areas, which are relevant to the issue of socio-economic development too:

A – Domestic public resources;
B – Domestic and international private business and finance;
C – International development co-operation;
D – International trade as an engine for development;
E – Debt and debt sustainability;
F – Addressing systemic issues; and
G – Science, technology, innovation and capacity building

Of these seven suggested action areas, it has been decided to briefly discuss action areas C (International Development Co-operation) and G (Science, technology, innovation and capacity building).

6.4.1 International Development Co-operation

The Report rightly confirmed that:

> International public finance plays an important role in complementing the efforts of countries to mobilise public resources domestically, especially in the poorest and most vulnerable countries with limited domestic resources.[19]

This work stressed the fact that countries should refrain from external borrowing; they rather should finance their projects, where possible, through the domestic microfinance system.

However, the Addis Ababa Action Agenda promised to strengthen their dialogue to enhance their common understanding and improve knowledge-sharing.[20] Indeed, there exists a dearth of international co-operation particularly among the neighbouring countries let alone knowledge-sharing. The only example that may be cited in relation to this issue is perhaps ASEAN, the Association of South-East Asian Nations. Sharing of knowledge between countries of more or less similar countries and co-operation among themselves are vitally important factors of socio-economic development of countries. The Agenda not only confirmed the importance of South–South co-operation but also welcomed:

> ... the increased contributions of South-South cooperation to poverty eradication and sustainable development. We encourage developing countries to voluntarily step up their efforts to strengthen South-South cooperation, and to further improve its development effectiveness in accordance with the provisions of the

---

[19]Addis Ababa Action Agenda, op. cit., at 26.
[20]Ibid.

Nairobi outcome document of the High-level United Nations Conference on South-South Cooperation.[21]

The Addis Ababa Agenda also rightly perceived the correlation between socio-economic development and the need for the protection of a clean environment. It stated, inter alia, that:

> We acknowledge that the United Nations Framework Convention on Climate Change and the Conference of the Parties thereto is the primary international, inter-governmental forum for negotiating the global response to climate change. We welcome the Lima Call for climate action and we are encouraged by the commitment of the Conference of the Parties to reaching an ambitious agreement in Paris in 2015 that is applicable to all parties and that reflects the principle of common but differentiated responsibilities and respective capabilities, in light of different national circumstances.[22]

6.4.2 Science, Technology, Innovation and Capacity Building

The Conference at Addis Ababa noted with concern the persistent 'digital divide' and the uneven innovative capacity, connectivity and access to technology, including information and communication technology within and between countries.[23] The Agenda emphasised that capacity development will be integral to achieving the post-2015 development agenda. The Addis Ababa Agenda is very ambitious. One can only hope that the international community co-operates in fulfilling this Agenda items.

6.4.3 The Role of International Trade in Development

Incidentally, it is important to point out that this Agenda, also included the role of international trade as an engine of development. It promised to continue 'to promote a universal, rule-based, open, transparent, predictable, inclusive, non-discriminatory and equitable multilateral trading system under the World Trade Organisation (WTO), as well as meaningful trade liberalisation'.[24]

Bi-lateral cross-border trade (which is popularly known as international trade even though the governing law of the contracts of import–export trade is usually the domestic law of one of the contracting parties, and not the principles of public international law) should be regarded as an engine of growth. Trade, whether domestic or transborder, entails activities in a number of sectors of an economy

---

[21]Addis Ababa Agenda, op. cit., at 28.
[22]op. cit., at 29.
[23]The Addis Ababa Agenda, op. cit., at 51.
[24]The Addis Ababa Agenda, op. cit., at 37.

(diversification), promotes skills in people (capacity building) and increases income and employment in a country. Eventually, with appropriate skills a country, through indigenous means, can become a major exporting country in various products and services. It also can make a country self-sufficient in certain sectors of her economy.

But trade must be regulated at both domestic and non-domestic levels. Each country should devise her own standards (quality) of products which cannot be below the level of the international standards. Thus, regulatory measures are needed to be enforced at a domestic level, and the Member States of the WTO should be engaged in a more pro-active role in standard setting and provide technical assistance to its Member States, whenever it might be sought by them. But enforcement of regulatory measures is a matter for each government. Currently, however, not all trade practices which are applied to cross-border trade are non-discriminatory, e.g., the most-favoured nation standard (MFN), and the standards of the national treatment. The important questions that should be raised are whether the MFN standard creates equality, and also whether it may be possible, from a pragmatic point of view, for developing countries to observe the national treatment towards private foreign investors at the cost of their national interest. This may not be the most appropriate context to elaborate on these issues, but briefly, despite certain efforts made through the intervention of UNCTAD which after considerable struggle was able to introduce Generalised Systems of Preferences (GSP) which provides some kind of financial relief to developing countries when they export selected products under a GSP system; generally speaking, the international community is required to do that for attaining commercial equality in a functional sense between trading partners rather than compulsorily relying upon the most-favoured nation (MFN) standard which does not create equality 'in fact' between these partners.[25] To justify the above argument, one is required to return to the origins of the MFN, which is not a compulsory standard of international economic law, but nevertheless widely used by trading States. According to Schwarzenberger:

> ... the principles of MFN and national treatment made their first appearance in international law proper in the commercial treaties concluded during the twelfth century between English and Commercial Powers and cities.[26]

Hornbeck however maintained that the phrase 'most-favoured nation' first appeared in commercial treaties towards the close of the 17th century.[27] According to him, with the growing internationalisation of commerce and

---

[25]See further S K Chatterjee, 'Forty Years of International Action for Trade Liberalization', 23 *Journal of World Trade* (1989) at 45–64.
[26]G Schwarzenberger, 'The Most-favoured Nation Standard in British State Practice', 22 *British Year Book of International Law* (1945) 96–121, at 96.
[27]S K Hornbeck, 'The Most-favoured Nation Clause (Part I)', 3 *American Journal of International Law* (1909) at 3.

navigation, it became a common practice for commercial nations to use this standard. He clearly described this practice when he stated that:

> During the nineteenth century, while international trade became world commerce, commercial treaties became so common that they now bind the trading nations in fine-meshed web. In these treaties the clause of the most-favoured nations was inserted with so few exceptions as to warrant its characterisation as the cornerstone of all modern commercial treaties.[28]

Thus, although an age-old standard, the MFN standard does not really create any equality between the trading partners. In addition, if the standard of the national treatment is to be observed by each host developing State, then their national interest may not be sufficiently protected, whereby the national industries operating in the same sector of the economy in which foreign entities are also operating, the national firms would not receive any preferential treatment in consequence of which they might be disinterested in staying in the sector of the economy concerned.[29]

The Economic and Financial Committee of the League of Nations also believed that a discriminatory trade policy would only assist the prospect of world peace recede.[30] The unsuccessful Havana Charter advocated the operation of the MFN clause as a means of avoiding discriminatory treatment between trading partners.[31] Interestingly enough, Part I of the General Agreement on Tariffs and Trade (GATT) was also based on the MFN standard; this was perhaps for two reasons: (a) without questioning its appropriateness as to whether an application of this would create equality; in fact, it, as a matter of historical practice, found it necessary to incorporate it in Part I of the Agreement; and (b) that it was a timely offer of a preferential trading arrangement made by the developed States to the newly-born de-colonised States.[32]

The effectiveness of this standard as a means of providing 'equality in fact' as opposed to 'equality in law' should be seriously considered by the international trading community. According to Schwarzenberger again, The MFN standard

> ... serves increasingly to provide proportional, rather than absolute equality between the beneficiaries.[33]

---

[28]Ibid.

[29]See further S K Chatterjee, 'Forty Years of International Action for Trade Liberalisation', op. cit.,

[30]League of Nations, *Commercial Policy in the Inter-Wars Period: International Proposals and National Policies* (1942) at 47–51.

[31]See further C A Wilcox, *A Charter for World Trade*, New York, Macmillan (1949).

[32]See further S K Chatterjee, op. cit., at 47.

[33]G Schwarzenberger, 'The Principles and Standards of International Economic Law', 117 *Recueil des Cours, The Hague Academy of International Law* (1966) I, 1–98, at 77.

Based on treaty-practices it may be stated that MFN clauses cover a range of subjects, namely, importation, exportation, transit rights, customs duties, navigational rights, etc.[34] MFN standard may take any of the following forms: conditional, unconditional, unilateral, reciprocal, absolute or relative. Preferences under the MFN standard is usually offered on a product-by-product or service-by-service basis.[35] The scope of this kind of preference is often determined by the grantor State. One should also consider the reason why MFN preferential standard is not part of customary international law or even a compulsory standard under international economic law. It is worth noting that in 1941, the US Department of State pointed out the limitation of this Standard in the following passage:

> It is to be admitted that the most-favoured nation principle alone, without a moderate level of non-discriminatory rates, is not sufficient of itself to promote a healthy international trade. The United States has since recognized this fact in the enactment of the Trade Agreement Act.[36]

Mutual preferential trading arrangements are congenial for both the parties to a bilateral treaty. The extent to which multilateral preferential treatment like that offered through the MFN standard is not really helpful; in practical terms, it is formed on the legal philosophy of equality in law. What is needed is equality in fact – the dilemma that equality in law presents is shown below by means of a diagram:

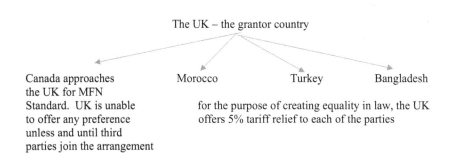

The UK – the grantor country

Canada approaches the UK for MFN Standard. UK is unable to offer any preference unless and until third parties join the arrangement

Morocco   Turkey   Bangladesh

for the purpose of creating equality in law, the UK offers 5% tariff relief to each of the parties

---

[34]For a discussion of the need for a wider application of the MFN Standard, see the *Report of the International Law Commission* (1969), vol II, UN DOC A/CN. 4/213.
[35]See further S K Chatterjee, op. cit., at 47.
[36]Memorandum of the Chief of the Division of Commercial Treaties and Agreements (Hawkins) to Assistant Secretary of State, Achison, 1 August 1941, *Foreign Relations* vol III, pp 19–21; cf M Whiteman, 14 *Digest of International Law*, at 749.

In this diagram, Canada is the strongest party, whereas Bangladesh is the weakest from an economic standpoint. Turkey would be next to Canada; Morocco would be next to Turkey. Each of these countries shown in the diagram is a textile producing country. Thus, in order to establish 'equality in fact', for example, if Canada is offered 5% tariff relief then, in order to establish equality in fact, the lesser countries in this example, should perhaps be allowed tariff concession in the following order:

Turkey – 6%
Morocco – 7%
Bangladesh – 8%

The reader is reminded that this is a mere example to establish the point about 'equality in fact' in transnational trade. Thus, instead of using the MFN standard, the international trading community should develop a non-discriminatory preferential trading system at the forum of the WTO. The Generalised Systems of Preferences (GSP) are also limited in nature in that the choice of products on which GSP is allowed are made by the Grantor States.[37]

Trade must be regarded as an engine of growth; growth stands for infrastructural development, which would include not only roads, railways and communication network but also basic education and health facilities for people and of course capacity building. One must reflect on the lack of progress owing to the employment of inappropriate policies whether for external reasons or internal factors. As has been stated earlier that political systems which are in most cases undemocratic combined with the idea of foreign-dependence of whatever nature, would be a primary cause of developing countries remaining developing. On the other hand, developing countries' aspirations of 'westernisation' as a 'quick fix' for development is wrong. If a country remains poor for a long time and operates a dictatorial form of government, she will experience large flow of emigration of human resources which has been the case for the last four decades, if not more.

So, how should one go for socio-economic development? Before putting forward any positive ideas, it would be better to enter certain negative points which one should avoid implementing in a development process. First, one should be aware of the limits of socio-economic development; these are now identified.

Limits of socio-economic development can be set by internal as well as external factors.[38] Whereas internal factors would include governmental policies and programmes and the opportunities to develop human resources, external factors would include, inter alia, over-reliance on foreign aid, transfer of inappropriate technology or creation of certain industries which would give rise to economic enclaves because of their traditional links with certain secure foreign markets in such a situation, diversification of economies does not take place; a kind of

---

[37]See further S K Chatterjee, 'Forty Years of International Action for Trade Liberalisation', op. cit.
[38]See further S K Chatterjee, *International Law of Development*, op. cit., at 200.

economic stagnation develops.[39] Then there is the practice of politicisation of socio-economic development. Hierarchical development may not be the most appropriate type of development process; it must be participatory – indigenous people must be engaged in the development process of their country. Underdeveloped state of affairs should not be treated as a hindrance or limit; they should, with pride, be engaged to develop what is not up to the expected level of standards.

6.5 Whether Socio-Economic Development May Be Achieved Through Rural Marketing

'Socio-economic development' is a multi-dimensional concept; obviously, in order to achieve it, a holistic approach to rural marketing would be essential. In line with the primary objective of this it is maintained that one of the means of developing rural economies in developing countries would be to motivate rural people, both male and female, in commercial activities which, it is believed, might create interest in them. By being so engaged, they will be able to interact with people, as a result of which their communication skills should be improved; they will also learn their work and take interest in it when combined with capacity building.

This theme need not be developed through any mathematical or statistical method. It is a question of making them feel that they are a very important part of their country, and that their contribution through their work is to be recognised by their country and that they also deserve recognition like all other people in the country. It has been reported in this work to emphasise the importance of developing the rural world in developing countries by and through the participation of the rural people rather than neglecting them altogether which makes them feel neglected.

Initially, rural marketing will present certain difficulties in breaking the ground. Below is shown some of the difficulties which the initiators of rural marketing might encounter in rural areas in the developing world:

- probably very scanty or even no data on any issue may be available;
- rural people in developing countries are generally unaware of the most recent developments in the world of business;
- scarcity of funds;
- scarcity of novel ideas;
- scarcity of the appropriate skills; and
- communication difficulties

---

[39]For guidance on this issue, see UNCTAD Draft Code of Conduct on Transfer of Technology, dated (1985); see also UN Commission on Transnational Corporations, *Transnational Corporations in World Development* (1983) sub-title: Acquisition of Technology at p. 50.

This cannot be a complete list; in other words, during the initial period, the trainers will be required to do the background work.

It has already been emphasised that the majority of the de-colonised countries, for whatever reasons, tend to disregard their rural areas, in consequence of which these areas and the people therein remain 'poor' from all senses of the term. Their aspirations are low; they are often the victims of prejudices carried by urban people in their own country – a situation that deserves the urgent attention of everybody concerned not only in the urban areas but also the public authorities too.

This has not happened as yet. It has therefore been suggested that the best and interesting way of changing the rural areas in the developing countries, in general, is by and through an effective socio-economic development process.

The road to achieving a satisfactory level of socio-economic development will initially be bumpy, but the rural people should eventually reach their goal. They must be made familiar with the required standards of goods or products, as the case may be, under the local legislation, and where possible, even to reach the standards recommended by the International Chamber of Commerce.

After the 'teething problems', so to say, are over, there is no reason why the rural people through experience buttressed by capacity building should not be able to contribute to a planned socio-economic development process in rural areas.

Rural marketing and sales techniques should not be confused with urban marketing and sales techniques. The following are some of the important factors, which rural marketing and sales forces should particularly consider:

- the attitudes and buying habits of the people in the rural areas concerned;
- their buying capacity;
- their average income;
- whether rural people should be initially part of the sales force or part of both sales and marketing forces;
- transport and communication systems, which should be gradually improved;
- rural branding of products which, in fact, should be an important contributing factor for encouraging rural people to participate in the development process in their geographical areas;
- a special finance act for sufficient financial allocation of funds to each of the rural areas in the country according to each of developing country's legislative process has to be enacted;
- rural people should be engaged in producing and/or manufacturing products according to the choice of the rural people to cater for the rural people; but gradually they should try to explore the urban markets;
- one may find numerous difficulties or rather unusual circumstances in promoting marketing and sales of products and small industries, in addition to the agricultural and textile industry sectors, but with the assistance of the Federal and State governments, where relevant, and training from people with experience in rural development, preferably from inside the country, should materialise the plan for socio-economic development in rural areas in the developing world.

6.6 Conclusions

The Millennium Development Goals and Targets for 2015 identified the following objectives of development:

- To increase the availability and expand the distribution of basic goods needed for living, namely, food, shelter, health, and physical protection for the peoples;
- To raise the standards of living of peoples in the country concerned; and
- To expand the range of economic and social choices so as to make them available to individuals by freeing them from servitude and dependence.

According to Todaro and Smith, the core values of development are sustenance, self-esteem and freedom.[40] Amartya Sen, a Nobel Laureate, believes that the 'capability to function' is what really matters in development.[41]

It has been stated earlier that too many theories already exist on development; but the progress on development on a global scale still remains abysmal. No global view on development will work; development has to be achieved through local (indigenous) means with the help of the local people. Each country's geographical, geophysical, socio-political circumstances are different. 'Westernisation' is not development. Having studied the local conditions, the means of achieving development must be determined. Africa, Asia and Latin America, in general (except Australia, Japan, New Zealand) are different from the Western World. Climatic conditions set a limit to a development process; in view of tropical climatic conditions, in general, certain diseases, namely, cholera, malaria, typhoid, etc. will have an adverse effect on the health of the human resources.

The role of private foreign investors (transnational corporations) in developing a country's economy may not be underestimated, but they should be invited for the purposes of deriving benefits from their investments. Economies should be clearly divided into three sectors: open, closed and open-closed. It is in the latter (open-closed) sectors, at least for the first few years, that private foreign investors should be invited on mutually agreed terms based on bi-lateral investment treaties between the host country and the country to which the transnational corporation belongs. In this connection the reader may like to consult the UN General Assembly Resolution of 1962 entitled Permanent Sovereignty over Natural Resources. 'Bargaining Power' is a false notion which has been dominating the business world for a very long time. It simply stands for the 'power to negotiate'; this power signifies brain power and the knowledge and skills needed for negotiating terms and conditions of investment agreements which would benefit both the parties.

---

[40]M P Todaro and S C Smith, *Economic Development*, Harlow, Pearson Publishers (2015) at 22.

[41]Amartya Sen, 'Development Thinking at the Beginning of the 21st Century' in *Economic and Social Development in the XXI Century*, Emmerij L (ed), Inter-American Development Bank and Johns Hopkins University Press, Washington DC (2003).

Developing countries should invite private foreign investors on BOT (Build, Operate and Transfer) basis whereby the foreign entity would be required to build the industry with the participation of the local people (direct source of capacity building) and manufacture high-quality products (and this way service industries may also be developed) which would cater for both the domestic markets of the host country and of the private foreign investor; the latter should also create export markets for the host country; then gradually, the industry would be run by both the parties on agreed terms and conditions. The other current practice of paying profits or royalty by private foreign investors or even by foreign public investors should be reviewed – they should agree to do business on 'countertrade' basis without carrying any prejudices against this method of doing business with foreign parties.[42] Some of the rich countries which do business on countertrade basis are Australia, many of the Middle Eastern countries, New Zealand, Russia and the UK. Developing countries should build their foreign hard currency reserves, rather than spending them, often unnecessarily. A clear private foreign investment policy should be developed by each developing country in addition to a screening policy whereby the intending private foreign investor might be inclined to enter into the country for making investment. They must also be provided protection according to their 'best ability' under public international law.[43]

In addition to the above, developing countries are required to develop their banking and insurance industries to make them reliable and attractive to private foreign investors. They should also develop confidence in the minds of private foreign investors as to the high standards of their judiciary which does not promote bias, and which is separable and separate from the country's Executive wing of the government. This is not to suggest that the current judiciaries in the developing world are below the international standards, but prejudices against them unfortunately prevail.

Having identified the basic factors of development, one may not turn a blind eye to the sheer realities that often hinder socio-economic development in a country. It has been stated earlier that peace and development go hand-in-hand, but the current world is 'dry' on peace. This has a direct adverse effect on the development process in a country. Furthermore, day-by-day, the world is becoming very technology-oriented. Can developing countries, in particular, their rural areas keep pace with the onward march of technology, and if they can, they will be required to spend very large amounts of funds. Additionally, technology is also widening the generational gap at a societal level. The older generation, in general, all over the world, are less advanced in technological knowledge than the younger generation in consequence of which the perception of 'socio-economic development' becomes different, that is, whether it should be technology-oriented or non-technology oriented. In the event of choosing the latter, developing countries will be even more losers. This is a huge dilemma for development.

---

[42]See further C Chatterjee, *Legal Aspects of Trade Finance,* London, Routledge (2008).
[43]See further AAPL.

There then exists the national security issues – the security of most of the countries, if not all, is now in a vulnerable position owing to the abuse of technology. In these circumstances, developing countries, like developed countries, are required to divert their resources, financial or otherwise to the security issues which will certainly adversely affect their development process. Thus, a high-level diplomatic solution is urgently needed to resolve this problem.

Application of technology for achieving development in most aspects of it, is undeniably useful, but given their financial capacity, in general, in most cases they will have to settle for used technology from the West, which would be less productive, unsuitable for manufacturing the most modern products, will pollute the environment and would not be cost effective as they will often need repair etc.; hence, the suggestion that they should nevertheless try to develop their indigenous technology. Technology would be essential for certain sectors, in particular, education, medicine and surgery, communications, transport including infrastructural industries, banking, shipping, etc. The transformation from manual means to technological means will take time, but it is achievable; but the caution must be entered that unless a country like India, for example, takes special interest in technological development, the technological gap between the developed and developing countries will remain in the foreseeable future.

Finally, the darker and the brighter sides to socio-economic development have been in simple words been summarised by Marcelo M Giugale in his book entitled *Economic Development: What Everyone Needs to Know* In his 'Concluding Thoughts' the author stated, inter alia, that[44]:

> Politics can make reforms difficult if not impossible, no matter how sensible and beneficial those reforms may be. Being technically right is not enough for change to happen.

He went on to say that:

> Despite all that, you were also told that we are witnessing, or about to witness, major transformations and, yes, major progress ... [governments and people are becoming closer to each other] Technology and information have given us powerful tools to help the poor and the excluded.[45]

---

[44]Oxford University Press, Oxford and New York (2014). At the material time, the author was the Director of Economic Policy and Poverty Reduction Programmes for Africa.
[45]op. cit., at 127.

Chapter 7

ICC International Code of Direct Selling, 2013

Abstract

This chapter deals with the principal features of the International Code of Direct Selling 2013 prepared by the International Chamber of Commerce on Marketing and Advertising. Having identified the Basic Principles of Direct Selling and the Ideal Conduct towards Consumers, this Code also details the conduct which should be shown towards direct sellers; in addition to their responsibility to and in the event of any breach thereof, the responsibility to be discharged by the direct sellers. That is why this Code of Conduct provides for special training for familiarisation of the important provisions of this Code. This Code intends to achieve a number of objectives, namely (a) the importance of responsibility and good practice in direct selling in any jurisdiction; (b) to respect consumer preferences and privacy and the need for consumer protection – as the days of *caveat emptor* are over – the onus of consumer protection has been passed on to the sellers of products and services; and (c) direct selling should be done with social and professional responsibilities.

Keywords: International Code of Direct Selling 2013; the basic principles of direct selling; responsibility; good practice; consumer protection

7.1 Introduction

This Code was prepared by the International Chamber of Commerce on Marketing and Advertising. It has been developed over four chapters, namely:

Chapter A: Basic Principles;
Chapter B: Conduct towards Consumers;
Chapter C: Conduct towards Direct Sellers; and
Chapter D: Responsibility, Substantiation and Implementation.

Rural Marketing as a Tool for National Development, 101–110
Copyright © 2024 Charles Chatterjee
Published under exclusive licence by Emerald Publishing Limited
doi:10.1108/978-1-83608-064-020241008

Although not all the Members of the United Nations belong to the International Chamber of Commerce for whatever reason(s), there is no reason why the non-members of ICC may not volunteer to observe the self-regulatory Codes published by it. Direct selling of products brings significant benefits to consumers, producing companies and of course, the society, be it urban or rural, in general. In view of the gradual high level of consumer awareness, direct sellers of products should be responsible; hence the need for self-regulatory Codes of Conduct which may be developed according to the needs of rural markets and the capabilities of rural sellers. An application of a self-regulatory Code of Conduct for direct selling, special training for familiarisation of the relevant provisions would be necessary and should simply confirm responsible sales obligations on the part of rural sellers which would eventually give rise to a concomitant effect on consumers. Observance of these Codes of Conduct provides confidence in the minds of consumers.

Historically, the first Code of Advertising Practice was issued by ICC in 1937; thereafter, it successively revised its Codes of Conduct in order to raise ethical rules in sales globally. According to the ICC, its Code of Direct Selling forms part of its normative system. The Consolidated ICC Code of Advertising and Marketing Communication Practice was published in 2006, and the Code of Direct Selling, which is a stand-alone document, is linked to it too.

The 2013 edition of the Code of Direct Selling was developed in close co-operation with the World Federation of Direct Selling Associations (WFDSA).

7.2 The Purpose and Scope of the Code

The primary purpose of this Code is to develop within the industry of direct selling a system of self-regulation and self-discipline, and even the courts may use it as a reference document within the framework of the country's applicable legislation. It is not by law alone that certain aspects of human conduct may be effectively regulated; hence the need for Codes of Conduct.

This Code intends to achieve a number of objectives:

- To highlight the importance of responsibility and good practice in direct selling in any jurisdiction;
- To respect consumer preferences, privacy and the need for consumer protection; in other words, the days of the old fashion maxim *caveat emptor* (buyer beware) are over; the onus of consumer protection has been passed to sellers of products and services. In England and Wales, the Consumer Rights Act, 2013 is worth referring to on this point.
- To enhance public confidence in direct selling; there exists a concomitant relationship between a high degree of public confidence in sales people and consumers;
- To promote competition by maintaining fair competition amongst direct sellers in the product(s);

- To resolve differences and disputes between the parties concerned, if any, through negotiation rather than court proceedings; and
- To minimise the need for governmental regulations or regulations from any other institutions of whatever nature.

This Code applies to all direct selling activities, not only actual sales but also their associated activities. The art of direct selling requires a particular type of seller with an effective communication ability and good manners. The seller's courteousness must be demonstrated. Special skills are required for telephone marketing and for the use of digital interactive media. The reader should look at chapters C and D of the consolidated ICC Code which has covered these issues. Direct selling companies and their agents should follow the standards of ethical conduct, which have been set by this Code.

7.3 Definitions

7.3.1 Direct Selling

It stands for selling products directly to consumers. Such an activity entails responsibility on the part of a direct seller. As stated earlier that in this process neither the manufacturing company of product(s) nor its agents can assume that the buyer should know what he/she or it is buying. Under English law, the doctrine of *caveat emptor* (buyer beware) has long been abolished. These are the days of 'seller beware' instead, so to say. In England again, such activities are now governed by the Consumer Rights Act 2013. Direct selling may take place even at a consumer's place of habitual residence, or by and through a local shop, the latter is a common phenomenon in rural areas.

Chapter A: Basic Principles
Article 1 provides the basic principles of direct selling. According to this Article, all direct selling must satisfy the following criteria: legal, decent, honest and truthful. Each of these criteria must be satisfied according to the local definitions developed whether by legal principles or by societal practices. This is when one of the impediments to successfully implementing the ICC Code stands; incidentally, this impediment may stand in the way of implementing other ICC Codes too. The probable solution to the problem has received attention in the Conclusions to this chapter.

This Article further provides that direct selling activity 'should' be 'carried out with a due sense of social and professional responsibility'. This is a universal appeal, but the fact remains how many business communities and entrepreneurs maintain 'business ethics'. The phrase 'direct selling would be carried out with due sense of social and professional activity' would clearly suggest that a high degree of ethics is expected of direct sellers and their performance in regard to these activities too. By referring to the basic theme of this work, it may also be stated that it may be much easier for unscrupulous direct sellers to take advantage of the lack of knowledge of the consumers in rural areas. Thus, these direct sellers must be specially trained in direct selling activities in rural areas, in developing countries, in particular.[1] The phrase '. . . a due sense of social and professional responsibility' requires marketing officers to satisfy their requirements particularly for direct selling of products in rural areas of developing countries. The more conscious the direct sellers are of their social and professional responsibilities, the more confidence will they develop in consumers. This is precisely what the third basic principle under Article 1 stands for.

Fair competition, according to Article B1 is the final basic principle of direct selling. Thus, an elementary conclusion may be drawn suggesting no monopolisation of direct selling would be permitted under the Code. This also suggests that consumers should have access to the competition/anti-competition laws of their governments.

Chapter B: Conduct towards Consumers
Chapter B of the Code deals with conduct towards consumers, which is a very important principle of direct selling. 'Conduct' in this context would include 'direct' and 'indirect' conduct of a direct seller. Under Chapter B there are 19 Articles. Each of these articles is now being briefly examined.
Article B1
This Article is concerned with 'fair' dealing with consumers. It should be pointed out at the outset that from a lawyer's point of view, the word 'fair' has no meaning, as it varies from human mind to human mind, and it takes away the predictability of judgements. There is no reason why this statement may not be applicable to the business communities either. However, the primary theme of this Article is simple – direct sellers must not provide misleading information to the actual and/or future consumers; or they should not explain the advantages and disadvantages of their product(s) in an ambiguous and unclear words; nor should they practise any unfair sales method(s). They must not also subject their consumers/customers to any pressure of any nature whereby they might feel themselves obliged to accept the product(s). There exists a difference between 'direct selling' and the act of pressurising the prospective consumers as subjects of market research. In no way should the direct sellers, and their agents abuse the trust of individual consumers, and take advantage of the age, the lack of understanding of the prospective consumer of the merits and defects of the product(s) whether owing to the lack of a general understanding of what the direct seller told him/her or owing to his/her unfamiliarity with the language used by them.

The drafting of Article B1 entitled Fairness is rather loose, but then, in order to fit the provisions in as many jurisdictions as possible, one is required to allow a degree of inarticulate expressions. Whereas in the Western part of the world, in general, the perception of 'fairness' seems to be higher than that which may be found, in general, in developing countries. The Consumers Rights Act 2013, for example, in the UK simply strengthens the position of consumers; thus, the sellers

---

[1]The author is fully informed of the fact that there does not exist any acceptable definitions of 'developed' and 'developing' countries. Roughly, colonised areas were described as 'developing' countries.

of products, whether by direct or indirect sales of them are required to conform to that legislation. In order to protect the rights of all consumers all over the world, all jurisdictions in the world should enact such a legislation, as that would be a step forward towards globalisation of consumer rights and duties.

Article B2 – Respect for Privacy

'Reasonable' is a relative term. The societal aspirations of societies often prove to be a determining factor for it. Furthermore, the wish of a particular buyer vis-à-vis a seller should be respected by the latter. The Code provides an example of what is meant by 'respect of privacy' when it states that a 'no selling sign on door' represents the wish of the buyer, and that a 'direct seller' should respect the wish of that buyer or he/she should not be disturbed whether by telephone calls or otherwise during what is commonly known as 'ungodly hours'. Demonstration or sales presentation should be stopped immediately by a direct seller if so requested by a prospective consumer. All such sellers should carry out 'any collection and processing of data' in strict compliance with Article 19 of the Consolidated ICC Code of Advertising and Marketing Communication Practice, 2006.

Article B3 – Identification

'Identification' in this context would imply a correct and authentic identification of the direct seller(s) and his/her/its affiliation with the company concerned. Obviously, this provision is meant for providing protection to the consumers against misrepresentation of their identities. These sellers should also clearly explain the purposes of their visits to the prospective consumers of their products and/or services. According to the Code, promotional literature, advertisement, etc. should contain the name, address and contact number (telephone) or email identification of the direct seller.

Article B4 – Accuracy

The terms of the offer should be clearly stated in order to ensure that the prospective consumer understands what is being offered, at what price and presumably the terms and conditions of payment; furthermore, the prospective consumer should also know what his/her legal obligations are in placing the order.

Article B5 – Truthfulness

Presentations and/or demonstrations of products should be done in a simple language which the prospective customers would easily understand; the use of the local language with which they may be familiar in these processes might prove to be very useful. In promoting their products, direct sellers should ensure that in no way, whether directly or indirectly, they mislead the prospective customers. These sellers should only make promises concerning the products of the company which they represent.

Article B6 – Explanation and Demonstrations

According to this Article the product offered should be described and shown to be exactly what the customer expected, therefore, any misleading word or the use of inaccurate description of the product, including the price of it and returning conditions once delivery has been made, would not be permissible.

Again, the Code has emphasised that the use of clear language in selling products by direct sellers is essential for a clear understanding of the quality and use of the product these sellers are about to sell. According to the Code, the seller must give the consumer an opportunity to read the entire contract without putting any undue pressure on him/her. It is therefore reiterated that contracts of sale must be written in the simplest possible language; there is no reason why a contract of sale should be written in legal language, unless of course, the use of certain technical words in the trade becomes inevitable, but in that case, the corresponding meanings of the terms should be given either in the form of footnotes or in brackets in the main text of the contract.

Article B7 – Order Form

Order forms to be delivered to the consumer should be in a written form, which should contain the name of the direct seller's company, the full name of the direct seller, his/her contact details and full address and contact details of the company the product of which he/she is trying to promote. The terms and conditions of sale should be clearly and legibly stated.

Article B8 – Comparisons, Denigration and Exploitation of Goodwill

Companies or sellers selling directly to the consumers should not make false comparisons which may misinform the buyers and would not be in line with the competition law. No unfair criticism or false impression of any seller, company, or product should take place. Sellers should not belittle the goodwill and logo attached to a company or a product.

Article B9 – Testimonials

Only genuine, verifiable and relevant testimonials or supportive documents may be submitted in support of the quality of goods but not obsolete or misleading documents or any kind of evidence in writing.

Article B10 – Guarantees

Guarantees or whatever other alternative expressions a direct seller may use, should disclose the terms and conditions of those instruments, including the limitations on consumer rights and remedies in clear terms which would easily be understood by the future consumers.

Article B11 – After Sales Service

A full description of after-sales service should be provided, where it may be offered. In the event of a consumer accepting the offer of an after-sales service, the direct seller should provide the precise and correct information as to how he/she may activate the service and communicate with the service agent.

Article B12 – Safety and Packaging

Companies should carefully package goods and products, including samples, in order to maintain the health and safety issues involved in it. Each country should have her health and safety legislation; however, the ICC Code of Direct Selling refers to Article 17 of its Consolidated ICC Code of Advertising and Marketing Communication Practice. This provision is very important for all customers, in particular, children and old people. Packaging material must not be harmful to the consumers and for the preservation of the environment.

Article B13 – Fulfilment of Orders

This Article provides that all orders must be effected within 30 days from the date the order was signed by the consumer. In the event of any undue delay occurring in supplying the product, the consumer should be informed immediately. Any request for cancelling an order and asking for refund, if due, should be acted upon in accordance with the contract. If, however, the delivery of the product/goods may not be stopped by the direct selling company, the consumer should be informed accordingly, and the consumer should be allowed to return the product/goods at the company's costs.

Article B14 – Substitution of Products

If the consumer's chosen product/goods becomes unavailable after the order has been placed, and that it became 'unavailable for reasons beyond the control of the direct selling company', another substitute product/goods may be supplied to the consumer provided of course he/she approved of it, and also provided that the replacement product is effectively similar to the original product ordered for by the consumer or of better characteristics and qualities, of the same price or lower than the original price of the product/goods ordered by the consumer. It must be liked by the consumer without any persuasion by the seller. The direct selling company will have an obligation to explain how the consumer may return the substituted product/goods, if disliked by him/her to the direct selling company at their costs.

Article B15 – Cooling Off and Return of Goods

Order forms used by direct selling companies and direct sellers should contain a cooling-off period, which would allow the prospective consumer to cancel the order within a specified period of time, and go through the procedure of getting a refund of any payment made or goods/products traded in. These terms should be clearly written on the order form in a simple language which would be understood by the prospective consumer.

Article B16 – Complaints

All direct selling companies should develop handbooks that should contain complaint handling procedures. The primary objective of this procedure is to consider complaints from consumers in an efficient and impartial manner. Thus, complaint handlers should be chosen very carefully. All complaints should be dealt with promptly and the decisions should be transmitted to the complainant(s) as soon as possible. The Code does not mention however that complainants should be heard also by the company panel or otherwise.

Article B17 – Price and Credit Terms

Sellers selling directly to the customer must show the terms and methods of payment clearly in their offer, and where the payments are to be made in instalments, the terms and conditions should be clearly explained to the customer. Furthermore, in such sales, the credit terms (if of course the customer agrees to these terms), the amount of initial deposit, the precise amount of subsequent instalment payments, and the differences in payments if bought on an instalment basis rather than on immediate total payment basis should be clearly shown on the offer letter.

Article B18 – Payment and Debt Collection

As a precautionary measure, the procedure for payments and that for collecting debts should be clearly stated in writing prior to signing any contract of direct selling so that the prospective consumer becomes aware of his/her obligations as to payments. According to the Code, no coerciveness should be shown to the debtors in the attempt to recover the money.

Article B19 – Referral Selling

Consumers should not be induced to effect any purchase by giving them an impression that if they can introduce new customers the sellers would reduce or even condone the price of the products they have purchased.

Chapter C: Conduct Towards Direct Sellers

The principal objective of this chapter is to identify the duties of direct selling companies vis-à-vis their direct sellers. Under English law, the business relationship between these two parties would be like that of a principal and agent; but the Code does not clearly state so. This chapter has been developed over 8 Articles and each of them has now briefly received attention.

Article C1 – Integrity

Direct sellers should be treated honourably and fairly by their companies and this requirement should also be applied to their new recruits. Furthermore, they should make their payments, or withhold them, where necessary, in a 'commercially reasonable manner'.

Direct sellers, on the other hand, should be provided with adequate training in order to enable them to perform their functions ethically. They should use the contents of the Code as a reference document as well as keep themselves informed of the contents of the Code. As a condition of the membership of the company's distribution network, the direct sellers should comply with the standards of the Code. This Article should be read with Article D6 entitled Respect for Self-Regulatory Decisions. In order to enable direct sellers to give their customers (consumers) all necessary information on the products and/or services they are also required to be fully informed by their companies of the characteristics of the goods and services offered by them.

Article C2 – Recruiting

Direct selling companies should not use any misleading or unfair recruiting practices; in addition, false promises or 'unverifiable factual representations' should not be made by these companies to their would-be direct sellers when recruited. By the same token, the scope and the benefits of selling opportunities should be presented to the prospective direct sellers truthfully.

The factors that are likely to affect any decision-making process of the direct sellers should be made clear to the prospective direct sellers in order to enable them to consider whether or not to accept any offer of employment, and if so, whether on distributorship or on commission basis.

Article C3 – Business Information

Information to be provided by direct selling companies to their prospective direct sellers concerning selling opportunities and related rights and obligations should be 'accurate and complete'. At the outset, direct selling companies should provide its direct sellers a written agreement/statement containing all terms and conditions of their engagement by the company concerned and that instrument should be signed by both the parties. Companies should update their sellers who are selling directly, of their legal responsibilities, including their licence requirements, if any, the regulations they would be bound by and their tax requirements.

Article C4 – Remuneration and Accounts

According to the Code, the direct sellers should receive periodic accounts from their companies informing them of sales, purchases, earnings, commissions, bonuses, cancelation of orders, etc. and other relevant data. All debts of the direct selling companies should be settled, as all withholdings must be made transparent. This is owing to the link between direct selling companies and their direct sellers.

Article C5 – Fees

No fees, namely entrance fees, training fees, franchise fees, etc. for joining the business should be high. The Code states that, where fees have been charged by a company to a direct seller it should be connected to the price of materials or products which have been provided in return.

Article C6 – Earnings Claims

Sales or earnings, which has already taken place or due to take place should not be distorted by the direct seller. Proofs of all sales and earnings should be correctly documented and kept.

Article C7 – Inventory

Large amounts of products should not bought or recorded by the direct sellers, and the following should be remembered when deciding on the right amount of product inventory:

- Whether predicted sales will be achievable;
- The environment prevailing in the market and the prospects of selling the products; and
- The policy of the company as to the return and refund of the products.

Article C8 – Termination

Upon termination of a direct seller's contract with the direct selling company, all unsold but saleable product inventory should be bought back by the latter, acknowledging the direct seller's actual costs minus a percentage of any reasonable handling charge incurred.

Chapter D: Responsibility, Substantiation and Implementation

The basic theme of this chapter is to remind the direct selling companies of their primary responsibilities for their direct selling activities.

Article D1 – Responsibility

First and foremost, their degree of responsibility should be commensurate with their position; and with this eventuality, the possibilities of observing the Code would be higher. Due care and diligence should be exercised by these companies and operated in such a way that they are able to fulfil their responsibilities.

The International Chamber of Commerce hopes that all sellers, individuals, companies, affiliated agencies, distribution companies and subcontractors should follow this Code.

Article D2

It has been confirmed in this Code that in order to operate direct selling activities in their entirety, which would also include audio or visual material originating from other sources, would not justify derogation from or not observing the rules of the Code.

Both the Articles D1 and D2 are concerned with the issue of responsibility of direct selling companies.

Article D3

A party who may have contravened this Code, should seek correction and appropriate redress, but even if the party's act has been corrected or appropriate redress has been granted, that would not excuse the contraventions.

Article D4 – Implementation

Independent self-regulatory bodies should be appointed by the parties concerned at both national and international levels to adopt and implement this Code and the principles embodied in it. The International Chamber of Commerce aspires that this Code should also be applied, where appropriate, by all organisations, companies and individuals, at all stages who may be involved in direct selling. However, it pointed out that the direct selling companies are primarily responsible for the enforcement of this Code against direct sellers. This chapter has tried to explain the principles of this Code published in 2013, however, further clarification can be requested from the ICC Code Interpretation Panel.

Article D5 – Substantiation

If a self-regulatory body needs to verify whether a direct selling activity is compliant with the principles of this Code, the facts should be provided to the authority concerned.

Article D6 – Respect for Self-Regulatory Decisions

Users of this Code should not become part of any direct selling activities which have been found to be unacceptable by any self-regulatory body or any dispute-resolution instrument.

Direct sellers should have a clause in their contracts asking them to follow all the relevant self-regulatory rules and to respect decisions and rulings made by such bodies.

7.4 Conclusions

Although the ICC International Code of Direct Selling was published by the International Chamber of Commerce about 7 years ago (2013), its provisions are still valid for direct selling companies and direct sellers. It is particularly relevant and indeed important for rural marketing which is the theme of this work.

It is important to reiterate that not only its basic principles, which have been explained in this section of this work, the section on 'Conduct Towards Consumers' and 'Conduct Towards Direct Sellers', are extremely important for rural consumers who often lack the product-knowledge as opposed to urban customers. The responsibility of direct sellers and the relationship between direct selling companies and direct sellers have been appropriately identified by the Code.

However, two almost unanswerable questions remain – whether the principles of the Code would be successfully implemented in all parts of the world, and the extent to which they will regard the Code as a legally binding instrument, even though its bindingness may be planned to be achieved by incorporating it in employment agreements and/or any other relevant documents.

Chapter 8

ICC Advertising and Marketing Communications Code, 2018

Abstract

This chapter examines the ICC Advertising and Marketing Communications Code of 2018. The primary themes of this Code are advertising and marketing communications. This is a lengthy Code – in addition to an Introduction, it has been developed over four chapters and two annexes. The 'technologically enhanced' marketing communications seem to have prompted the International Chamber of Commerce to draft this Code of Conduct.

This Code emphasised the self-regulatory Codes of Conduct in the hope that self-regulatory codes of conduct should convince customers of their social responsibility. This Code also believes that high sense of social responsibility will achieve the principal purpose of it. This Code should be more useful if the member States take it seriously and implement its provisions in their own interests.

Keywords: Technology; communications; business communities; social obligations; promotional

8.1 Introduction

This is one of the Codes that ICC has published on the topic of advertising and marketing communications, and which it is extremely relevant to the main theme of this work. The Code's sub-title, Building Consumer Trust Through Responsible Marketing, is also very significant in the context of this work. This is a rather lengthy Code, and in addition to an Introduction it has been developed over four Chapters and two Annexes. In view of the length of this Code, it has been decided to summarise the basic features of it.

Rural Marketing as a Tool for National Development, 111–131
Copyright © 2024 Charles Chatterjee
Published under exclusive licence by Emerald Publishing Limited
doi:10.1108/978-1-83608-064-020241009

The rapid growth and application of technology, which have led to evolving 'technologically enhanced' marketing communications, seem to have prompted the International Chamber of Commerce (ICC) to draft this Code of Conduct. In the Introduction to the Code, it identified the correlation between effective markets and economic development, which would eventually bring significant benefits to consumers, corporate entities and societies in general.

Advertisements for and marketing of products should be carried out respectively, and the Code emphasises the importance of self-regulatory codes of conduct, which should convince customers of 'the business community's recognition of its social obligations'; one of the foundations of corporate social responsibility and consumers' rights. The importance of self-regulatory codes of conduct should be appreciated by the national chambers of commerce, which should also keep a vigilant eye on their implementation.

This Code published in 2018 is about creating a proper framework to legalise marketing practices. One of the important features of this Code is that it clearly distinguishes between objective of codes of conduct and the role of legislation in achieving regulated markets. This Code rightly pointed out that the main objectives of codes is to set standards of ethical conduct; thus, these instruments should not be concerned with legal requirements; the ethical conduct of the business communities should respect them as legally binding instruments. This does not mean however that there is no room for legislation in marketing and advertising activities; these activities must also satisfy the legal requirements expressed through legislation. Ethical guidelines would be concerned with 'good' and 'bad' of a product/service; whereas legislative guidelines are to be implemented for achieving the minimum; ethical codes should be more effective in achieving social responsibility – they do not aim at any minimum standards; the more ethical is a mind, the more conscientious service would be rendered to customers.

As to the purpose of the Code, ICC maintains that this Code would be treated as an instrument of self-regulation of both commercial and non-commercial forms of advertising and communications. It also hopes that courts may refer to it and it may be used internationally. This Code is intended to achieve the following objectives:

- Advertising and marketing communications across the world should be based on responsibility and good practice;
- Marketing communications should enhance public confidence (that is, by providing a true, and non-misleading account of products/services), to respect privacy and consumer preferences and to demonstrate special responsibility in regard to marketing communication, which might be read by children and non-adults;
- Those who are engaged in marketing communication would be required to comply with Article 19 of the UN International Covenant on Civil and Political Rights, as to the use of words and terms, which would not be contrary to the local sense of decency; and
- To lessen the need for detailed governmental and/or inter-governmental legislation/regulations to provide effective solutions to consumer protection issues; here also the local norms of consumer protection based on their aspirations may have to be observed.

This Code has been developed over four Chapters:

Chapter A: Sales Promotion
Chapter B: Sponsorship
Chapter C: Direct Marketing and Digital Marketing Communications
Chapter D: Environmental Claims in Marketing Communications

This ICC Code should be read in conjunction with other current relevant ICC Codes, such as:

- ICC International Code of Direct Selling;
- ICC/ESOMAR International Code at Market, Opinion and Social Research and Data Analysis
- ICC Principles on Responsible Deployment of Electronic Product Codes;
- ICC Framework for Responsible Food and Beverage Communications;
- ICC Framework for Responsible Environmental Marketing Communications; and
- ICC Framework for Responsible Marketing Communications of Alcohol

Application of the provisions of this Code is subject to certain limitations, namely:

- announcements in press releases, media statements;
- information given in the product labels;
- public policy and corporate social responsibility programme statements, other than when a statement appears as a claim in a marketing communication; and
- Educational or entertainment communications that are not proposed to be covered by this Code.

The Code has also pointed out that marketing communications should be pitched in a way that the consumers to whom they are addressed clearly understand what the sellers are trying to convey.

8.2 An Analysis of the Code

Under the Part entitled General Provisions and Definitions on Advertising and Marketing Communications (Articles 1–26) the following have been identified by the ICC, and these are now briefly discussed.

Basic Principles (Article 1). It has been mentioned that marketing communications should be 'legal, decent, honest and truthful', and when being prepared a sense of social and professional responsibility should be borne in mind; they must not also impair public confidence in marketing. Behind these basic principles remains the pre-requisite of a high level of public awareness, which has been emphasised in this work, and which is a typical malaise in the rural areas particularly in developing countries. The term 'social and professional responsibility' provokes controversy. It is closely related to the existence of a high level of public awareness of these responsibilities.

That a high sense of social responsibility (Article 2) should be demonstrated through marketing communications may not be questioned; however, the definition of social responsibility would vary from society to society, and that no central body in the world may regulate/govern this issue. Modes of marketing communications have a significant role to play vis-à-vis the issue of social responsibility. When marketing communications are effected through pictures or artworks, often the principle of social responsibility is violated, and these pictures and artworks travel across national boundaries. Although, in theory, jurisdictional prohibitive measures exist; unacceptable pictures and artworks, nevertheless, tend to find their way into the legitimate markets. An urgent international action is necessary on this issue.

Some of the other basic principles mentioned in this Code, namely, decency, honesty and truthfulness (Articles 3, 4 and 5) are valid in the context of direct marketing in particular. However, the problems with the principle of 'decency' have been touched upon in the previous paragraph. One of the core objectives of this work has been that in promoting marketing in rural areas, no advantage should be taken by marketing agencies and their representatives of the lack of experience or knowledge of the rural people. This is where communication of knowledge through media proves to be essential.

The issue of truthfulness (Article 5) has already received attention in discussing the other Code entitled ICC International Code of Direct Selling, 2013. However, it should nevertheless be added that marketing communications should be free of ambiguity, exaggeration, which are, in effect, likely to mislead the consumer even in respect of copyright and industrial property rights (e.g. patents, trademarks, designs, trade names, etc.), official recognition of statement, awards received by the corporate entity concerned and their contributions to charitable causes.

All claims which may be made in marketing communication should be capable of substantiation (Article 6). All marketing communications should be distinguishable irrespective of the type of media used, and the basic commercial purposes of these communications should be transparent (Article 7), like the identity of the marketeer (Article 8) by providing its contact information. Marketing communications should not misuse technical or scientific data or even terminology by exaggeration of facts, the validity of a product claim (Article 9), false or misleading use of scientific terminology or vocabulary which would confound the prospective consumers, and in particular, the less knowledgeable and inexperienced consumers.

Any free items, as an incentive to purchase a product, such as free gift may be offered without any obligation. In the event of making any 'linked' offers, that is, combined with the purchase of another product, the related marketing communication should ensure that the total cost of buying the products has not been increased with a view to covering all or part of the cost of the offer (Article 10).

Marketing communications should not state directly or by implication that their 'guarantee' or any other expression having substantially the same meaning, which would be more extensive than that provided by law.

Marketing communications containing comparisons with similar products should be drafted in a way which would not mislead consumers, and points of comparison should be fact-based, and should also be capable of being substantiated, when necessary (Article 11).

Marketing communications should not be drafted and publicised in a manner which may have a denigrating effect on any person or group of persons, organisation or institution of any category or even professions (Article 12). Marketing communications must be genuine and verified. All sponsored endorsements should be supplied by appropriate disclosures (Article 13).

Such communications should not be personal unless permission has been granted by the person concerned nor should they be drafted in a way which might give the impression of the company's product(s) being endorsed by him/her (Article 14). Similarly, such communications should not use the name, logo, trademarks, etc. of another organisation, the ulterior motive of which is to take advantage of the latter organisation's goodwill (Article 15); nor should they imitate such communications from other firms, whether in the form of general layout, text, artwork, music, etc. whether from the local jurisdiction or overseas (Article 16). Such communications should not be developed in a way the intention of which is to disregard the health and safety issues recommended by the local national standards. Safety risks to which children, in particular, might be victims, should be clearly stated, and if necessary, by the use of pictures, sound, etc. (Article 17).

This Code has allocated a separate section to Children and Teens and developed certain general principles too (Article 18.1 and Article 19.4 in particular) which very rightly states that special care should be taken in regard to marketing communications 'directed to or featuring children or teens' (*General Principles –* Article 18.1). Products that are considered to be illegal and harmful or otherwise unsuitable for children should not be advertised in media by specifically targeting them. With regard to prohibition of marketing communications directed at children in relation to food and alcohol beverages, which would damage their health, the ICC has also developed a Framework for Responsible Food and Beverage marketing communications.

Marketing communications should not exploit the lack of experience or credulity of children, particularly, when demonstrating the level of performance of a product, and its use, and to that effect, marketing communications should not:

- mention the level that a child should be at to assemble or use a product. The ulterior reason for it would be to increase the sale of the product;
- overstate the description and the performance of the product;
- not tell the buyer whether he/she needs to buy any extras to ensure that the product works; and
- nothing should be drafted in any ambiguous form; they should be written in words, pictures or diagrams, which would be easily understood by children.

These communications should not be drafted in a way, which may cause harm to children or teenagers both physically and morally, and these communications should not give rise to the children or teenagers to engage in any form of dangerous activities (Article 18.3). According to Article 18 (3), sub-paragraph (2) marketing communications should not force children, teenagers or their parents to buy a product, which will make them feel superior or give them an advantage over other children or teenagers. These communications should not directly appeal to children so that they convince and sway their parents or guardians, as the case may be, to buy products for them. Prices of products should not be lowered whereby the children or teens, or parents may be persuaded to buy those products. Furthermore, marketing communications should not encourage children or teens to contact them for the purpose of buying them; instead, they should encourage them to obtain the consent of their parents or guardians, or otherwise require their parents to contact the communicator to ascertain the quality, merits and disadvantages, including harmful hazards, if any, of the products (Article 18.4).

As regards protection of children's personal data, the Code provides that:

- Children should be encouraged to obtain their parents' permission prior to their disclosing their personal data by whatever means, and it is for the marketing communicators to ensure that such permission has been given by their parents/guardians;
- It is only with the consent of the parents/guardians that the essential and necessary data should be allowed to collect;
- Consent of the parents/guardians would be required to collect any personal data from children and use them in any form of marketing communications and address them to children's parents and other members of their families; and
- No disclosure should be made to third parties on any form of personal data of children unless parents/guardians have given their consent to do so. 'Third parties in this context does not include agents or others who provide technical or operational support to the marketeer'.

Article 19 of the Code contains ICC's guidelines as to data protection and privacy of individuals providing such data. In collecting personal data, individuals from whom data would be collected, should be informed of the purposes of collecting his/her data and whether these may be transferred to a third party, excluding agents or anyone providing operational support, for whatever purposes. In the event of failing to inform the individual concerned of the purpose of collecting his/her personal data, according to the Code, it should be done as soon as possible thereafter.

Personal data should be collected only for 'specified and legitimate' purposes, and should be used only for those purposes, and for those purposes only. These should be collected only to the extent they may be necessary for the purposes for which they may be collected (not excessive) and should not be preserved for longer than is required for the purpose(s). In order to prevent any illegal access to them, suitable security measures should be in place, and in the event of transferring these data to a third party, the originator of them should ensure that the latter has an 'equivalent level of security measures'.

One must ensure that there is a privacy policy in place when collecting personal data for any form of marketing communication; and that should be readily available to customers (Article 19.5). The issue of consumer rights has received attention in *Article 19.6* of the Code. According to it, appropriate measures should be taken to ensure that consumers understand the following:

- their right to opt out of direct marketing list;
- their right to opt out of 'interest-based' advertising;
- to opt for 'general direct preference services';
- to prohibit the marketing communicators concerned not to make their personal data available to third parties for the latter's marketing purposes; and
- to request the marketing communicators to rectify incorrect personal data, which they may be holding on their system.

The Code mentions that when transferring personal data reasonable steps should be taken to ensure that adequate security measures are in place in order to protect the data protection rights of the client concerned. In this connection the Code recommends the use of the 'ICC model clauses covering agreements between the originator of the marketing list and the processor or user in another country' (Article 19.7).

The cost of communication to consumers for accessing messages should be made clear to them in a clear manner. Responses to communications from consumers should be made promptly. Calls should not be charged until the consumer may begin to fulfil the purpose(s) for which the calls were made (Article 20). Under this Code, consumers should not be asked for payment of unsolicited products (inertia selling) (Article 21). Marketing communicators should not appear to condone or encourage actions which would contravene the law, self-regulatory codes or the generally accepted 'standards of environmentally responsible behaviour' (Article 22). This issue has received further attention in a subsequent section of this chapter.

Article 23 of the Code deals with the issue of responsibilities of marketeers in relation to marketing communications of their products. In fact, upon a critical analysis of the provisions of this Code, it would appear that the underlying reason of most of them is to make marketeers aware of their responsibilities, direct or indirect in regard to marketing communications. Article 23 simply identifies some of the specific responsibilities of marketeers in respect of marketing communications.

According to this Article, this code-based responsibilities apply to other related participants, such as market influencers, bloggers, affiliate networks, data analysts, artificial intelligence used for marketing communication. Care should be taken by agencies and others when preparing marketing communications so that they work in line with the sellers responsibilities.

Similar responsibilities should be performed by other related institutions, namely, publishers, media owners, contractors, etc. None of these institutions should publish communications which might be misleading to the public. Similar responsibilities should also be performed by the employees who may be employed by any of these institutions/firms. The provision of this Code applies to all forms of marketing communication (the latter would include testimonials or audio or visual materials which may originate from other sources) (Article 23).

Even though an act of contravention by any of the parties concerned with marketing communication may have been subsequently corrected and appropriate redress thereof have been provided to the injured party, the contravention may not be excused (Article 24).

The ICC hopes that relevant local, national and/or regional self-regulatory organisations would adopt and implement this Code. To this end all concerned with marketing communication should be trained so as to be familiar with the provisions of this Code; one of the primary objectives of which being to satisfy the needs of consumers and to ensure that in the process of introducing their products consumers have not been misled, directly or indirectly, and appropriate channels of complaints must be established, and compensation must be paid for, where necessary (Article 25).

In the event of a regulatory body finding the material or text of a marketing communication unacceptable, that material or text of the communication should not be allowed to be published. The parties to the Code are asked to include a statement which would compel them to follow the relevant rules and decisions of the appropriate self-regulatory body if they fail to do so.

Finally, the State authorities that do not have any effective self-regulatory codes and arrangements in place are encouraged by ICC to pursue its current Code on Advertising and Marketing Communications (2018 edition).

8.3 Part II of the Code

Part II of the Code consists of four Chapters: A, B, C and D. *Chapter A* is concerned with sales promotion which is now briefly discussed. Whereas 'marketing' is a concept the main objectives of which are to conceive ideas as to how to promote a product, and the techniques of informing prospective customers as to the dimensions and characteristics of the product in order to enable them to decide on it, 'sales' entails an implementation activity of those conceived ideas. However, sales people are also required to ensure that in their sales activities, they do not mislead the customers as to the quality of their product(s) and answer all questions honestly which may be raised by prospective customers, bearing in mind that in the current business climate, customers are very conscious of their rights, and the majority of them would follow the 'value for money' concept. Sellers of products and services have a special responsibility to protect the less-informed customers.

As to the scope of this Chapter (Chapter A), the Code states that it applies to marketing devices and techniques whereby products would seem to be more attractive compared to the similar products on sale in the market(s). The provisions of this Chapter shall apply irrespective of the forms of distribution, and they shall also apply to sales and trade incentive promotions. Although promotions are usually temporary activities, the provisions of this Chapter would nevertheless apply to long-term and even permanent use of promotional techniques.[1] This Chapter covers all forms of sales promotion, including:

- 'premium offers of all kinds;
- reduced prices and free offers;
- the distribution of stamps coupons, vouchers and samples;
- charity-linked promotions;
- prize promotions of all kinds, including incentive programmes; and
- promotional element used in connection with other marketing communications, such as direct marketing or sponsorships'.[2]

But it does not cover the routine distribution of product supplement or accessories of a non-promotional nature.[3]

Article A1 – Principles Governing Sales Promotions
- customers should be dealt with fairly and honourably during sales promotion activities;
- the most reasonable expectation of the consumer emanating from promotional material; thus, all sales promotions should be prepared accordingly;
- the management of sales promotions and any obligations arising therefrom should be promptly and efficiently dealt with;
- transparency of the terms and conditions of all sales promotions should be paramount;
- unfair sales promotions which might harm competitors and other traders should not be allowed; and
- sales promotions should not be brought into disrepute by any activities of promoters, intermediaries or any others who might be involved in these activities.

Article A2 – Terms of the Offer
The techniques of promoting sales should be devised in a way which would be easy for the consumer to identify the terms of the offer including its limitations, and care should be taken to ensure that the value of the promotional product is not exaggerated nor do they 'obscure or conceal the price of the main product'.

---

[1]See p. 20 of the Code.
[2]Ibid.
[3]Ibid.

Article A3 – Presentation
No attempt should be made to mislead the prospective customers in presenting sales promotion information. All presentations of sales promotion activities should comply with the General Provisions of the Code.

Article A4 – Administration of Promotions
In order to meet the customers' expectations, proper resources and supervision together with suitable precautionary measures should be in place, particularly,

- the provisional item should be available in sufficient quantity to meet the anticipated demand; if delay in providing promotional materials proves to be unavoidable, the prospective consumers should be informed immediately, and if purchases are conditional upon receiving promotional material first, then sales people must ensure that these materials are made available to the prospective customers in appropriate numbers;
- the main features of the promotional items offered and whether there is any time-limit for acceptance;
- are these age-related and/or geographical and the availability of the items;
- where a monetary alternative would be available, such as vouchers or stamps, then the actual value must be clearly shown;
- full name and address of the seller promoting the goods must be provided in order to address complaints;
- if the promotional items are supporting any charity, then it must be made clear to the consumers the amount of money that will be given to the charity;
- Faulty goods or insufficient services should be corrected, or the customer should be compensated for by immediately reimbursing the purchase cost upon request;
- By the same token, in order to protect the interests of both consumers and marketeers and sales people, complaints against the latter should be dealt with effectively and as promptly as possible.

Article A5 – Safety and Suitability
All parties involved in promotional activities must feel safe and not be exposed to any harm or danger. In accordance with the General Principles of this Code marketeers should be socially responsible and ensure that unsuitable and inappropriate materials do not reach children.

Article A6 – Presentation to Consumers
Presentation to prospective consumers should be made in a language which would be easily understood by them. The prospects of their winning prizes should not be overstated. The Code then lists out the items of information with which prospective customers should be familiar. According to the Code, where relevant, information should include:

- clear instructions as to how to obtain or participate in a promotional offer, for example, conditions for obtaining promotional items, whether with or without any financial liability or conditions for taking part in prize promotions;
- the principal features of the promotional item(s) offered;

- whether promotional offers are subject to any time limit for acceptance;
- whether these offers contain any restrictions or participation, be they age-related or geographical or subject to the availability of the promotional items;
- where a monetary alternative would be available, whether in the form of vouchers or stamps, the actual monetary value should be clearly stated to the prospective customers;
- any costs related to shipping, and handling of goods, and the methods of payment for such costs; and
- for identification purposes, the full name and address of the seller who is promoting the goods should be provided in order to address complaints.

In the event of the promotions claiming to support any charity, prior to the completion of the purchase, the consumers should be informed of the amount of money that would be set aside for that purpose.

8.3.1 Information in Prize Promotions

According to this Code if a sales promotion includes a prize promotion, then the prospective customers should be made aware of it and relevant information should be given to them, if so required, but to provide information to them may not be conditional, for example, purchasing the main product, the following should be clearly stated:

- a clear provision showing the eligibility criteria for participation in the prize promotion exercise;
- whether any costs involved for whatever purposes if a prospective customer wishes to participate in the prize promotion exercise;
- any restrictions on the number of entries;
    how many prizes and their values to be awarded, and whether the winner will get any reduction in the price of the goods;
- whether there will be a skill contest, and if so, what the contest will be about, and the conditions applied to judging the performance of the participants;
- the process of selecting the award of prizes;
- the competition closing date;
- the date of publication of the results, and the means of communicating them to the contestants;
- the tax liability, if any, of winners of the prize;
- the time frame by which a successful contestant would be allowed to collect his/her prize;
- the composition of the jury, if a jury is involved in the prize awarding contest; and
- any plans and terms and conditions thereof to use winners' names or winning contributions after the event, if any.

Article A7 – Presentation to Intermediaries
Sales promotion should be presented to intermediaries in such a way that they are able to evaluate the services and understand the degree of commitments required of them. They should have adequate details in regard to the following:

- the scope of the promotion, including the duration of the promotion period;
- the presentation of the promotion to the potential customers;
- the terms and conditions related to participation;
- the agents' financial obligations; and
- particular organisational tasks required of them.

Furthermore, where relevant, the closing date or time-limit should appear on the external cover of products indicating 'promotional offers'.

Article 8 – Particular Obligations of Promoters
When planning sales promotions, due regard should be paid to the valid interests of intermediaries and importance should be given to their decisions where relevant. Particular attention has been paid to respect the loyalty that might exist between employees and their employers. The Code states that the interests of all parties, employees, employers, intermediaries and consumers should be taken into account when designing and implementing any promotional and incentive schemes.

This Code also provides for the rights of intermediaries' employees if they are going to be involved in the promotional activities, and in that event the obligations lie with the intermediaries to invite their employees to introduce to them the techniques of promotional activities. The prospective employee has the obligation to seek and receive the permission of his/her employer prior to participating in the promotional process.

All goods, including promotional items, should be delivered to the intermediary concerned bearing in mind the time-limit set on promotional offer(s). Where sales promotion involves an active co-operation of an intermediary and/or the latter's employees, consideration should be given to the fact that such relationship does not prejudge any contractual relationship which may exist between the intermediary and the consumers.

Under 'particular obligations of intermediaries', the Code refers to honesty and misrepresentation (*Article A9*) which are self-explanatory.

Article 10 – Responsibility
The final responsibility of any form of sales promotion lies with the promoter/seller; thus, the responsibility for observing this Code falls on him/her/it.

8.4 Sponsorship

8.4.1 Chapter B – Sponsorship, Etc.

This chapter is addressed to sponsorship, both commercial and non-commercial, relating to corporate image, brands, products, etc. The extent to which the principle of corporate social responsibility is observed by a sponsor is to be considered when referring to sponsorship.

Sponsorship in this Code refers to any commercial agreement which would mutually benefit both the sponsor and the sponsored. Such agreement would also offer financial or other support for certain direct or indirect benefits between the sponsor's products or brands and a sponsorship property in return for rights to promote such association.

Article B1 – Principles Governing Sponsorship
Contractual obligations are the basis for all sponsorship. This Code also emphasises the need for incorporating the contractual terms and conditions as clearly as possible. Furthermore, as it is a contractual undertaking, it points out that the terms and conditions should be based on good faith, a principle of the Law of Contract which may be found in all principal legal systems. The Code also states that the decision of the value of the sponsorship rights rests on the sponsored parties.

Article B2 – Autonomy and Self-Determination
This means that the sponsored party has the freedom to manage its own activities provided of course, in so doing it does not detract from its contractual obligations.

Article B3 – Imitation and Confusion
Sponsors and sponsored and other related parties should avoid imitation of products as such products might cause confusion in the minds of consumers. This is also an issue under Intellectual Property Law of the jurisdiction concerned.

Article B4 – Ambushing of Sponsored Properties
As the word 'ambushing' suggests, no party to a sponsorship agreement should mislead others by failing to disclose the sponsored properties.

Article B5 – Respect for the Sponsorship Property and the Sponsor
Special care should be taken by the sponsors to protect all contents of the sponsorship property be they artistic, cultural or sporting, and should not use their position to adversely affect or damage the reputation of the sponsored party or the sponsorship property. Neither party should do anything to damage the image, trademarks or goodwill of the parties.

Article B6 – The Sponsorship Audience
This Article should be read with Article B4 above. The participants and viewers at any event should be clearly informed of any existing sponsorship. In this context, the professional ethics of the sponsored party should be rigidly followed.

Article B7 – Data Capture/Data Sharing
The provisions of Article 19 would be applicable, where personal data might be used in connection with sponsorship.

Article B8 – Artistic and Historical Objects
Artistic and historical objects and public interests of them must be respected at all times by the sponsors. This is an issue which should really be incorporated into the sponsorship agreement.

Article B9 – Social and Environmental Sponsorship
At the point of planning and organising a sponsorship, both the parties should consider the potential societal and/or environmental impact of the sponsorship. In this respect, they may also take into consideration the principles set out in the ICC Business Charter for Sustainable Development (available from www.iccwbo.org).

Article B10 – Charities and Humanitarian Sponsorship
Sponsorship of charities and other humanitarian causes should be undertaken after a thorough research to fathom the extent of care and sensitivity of the society concerned and also for the purpose of ensuring that a sponsored party, when performing its activities towards those causes, is not adversely affected.

Article B11 – Multiple Sponsorship
In the event of appointing several sponsors, the rule of concluding individual sponsorship agreements should be followed; where however, special rights and duties are to be incorporated into such contracts, there is no reason why they should not be so included with reasons thereof. Each individual sponsor's special needs should also be taken into account.

Article B12 – Media Sponsorship
Sponsors should not influence the contents of media properties sponsored by them as it can weaken the editorial independence of the broadcaster and/or the programme producer unless the sponsor becomes the programme producer or co-producer or financier. The sponsors must ensure that the sponsored media properties have been clearly identified at the beginning, during and/or at the end of the programme. This should also apply to online materials.

Article B13 – Responsibility
Mutual benefit is the basis for sponsorship agreements; they must also observe the Code individually and jointly. Third parties taking part in a sponsorship agreement are also responsible, in accordance with Article 23 of the General Provisions in order to ensure their compliance with the Code.

8.5 Direct Marketing and Digital Marketing Communication

8.5.1 Chapter C – Direct Marketing and Digital Marketing Communication

Chapter C should be read in conjunction with the General Provisions and Definitions on Advertising and Marketing Communications and the Introduction regarding interpretation, jurisdiction and relationship with the law.[4]

This Chapter applies to parties involved in direct and digital marketing system including their marketing communications activities. In the context of this work, it may be maintained that most of the marketing communications in the rural areas in developing countries, in general, would during the initial period, be non-digital. However, whatever form or shape the marketing communication system may adopt, the ethical conduct in the process should be followed by all concerned.

The Code pointed out that:

> Recommendations on best practice for customer redress and dispute resolution in online business can be found in the ICC documents 'Putting it Right' and 'Resolving Disputes Online'.[5]

Article C1 – Identification and Transparency
Marketing communications and subject descriptions should be accurate and according to the Code, '... the commercial nature of the communication should be transparent' to the customer. No product endorsement or review should say or imply that it is from an individual consumer or independent body. Marketeers of the products should ensure that the contents of social network site are in accordance with the rules and standards expected of commercial behaviours. Marketeers should be absolutely transparent in regard to the product(s) they may offer. Thus, they should not sacrifice honesty and clarity in introducing their products.

Article C2 – Identity of the Marketeer
The identity of the marketeer or the operator should be clearly stated to the consumer in order to enable him/her/them to have access to the provider(s) of the product(s). Thus, the consumer should be made aware of the full identity of the marketeer/seller, when the product is delivered.

Article C3 – The Offer
The consumer should be clear about the terms and conditions of all offers made to him/her, and any requirements arising from the offer should be promptly dealt with. The rules of Sales Promotion must be observed when offers involving promotional items are being made (Chapter A).

---

[4]At p. 30 of the Code.
[5]Available from www.iccwbo.org

Article C4 – Presentation
The essential features of an offer should be stated in a simple language. In the event of a product entailing another product for the use of the former, the consumer should be informed of the need for a second product prior to his/her purchasing it. Consumers should be given a clear idea as to the steps they might require to fulfil prior to their placing an order and the formalities of conducting a contract. A marketeer should promptly notify a prospective consumer whether his/her offer has been accepted or rejected.

In respect of software or other technical devices, the marketeer should not cancel or obscure any material factor. A consumer should have all the information in relation to a product or technical device, including all the related costs, where relevant, before making any commitment.

Article C5 – High Pressure Tactics
Any form of intense pressure or harassment should be avoided by the seller to persuade consumers to sign up to an offer, particularly if the terms and conditions of purchasing that product cannot be confirmed.

Article C6 – Respect for Public Groups and Review Sites
Respect should be shown for the rules and standards of acceptable commercial behaviour if they are mentioned in the terms and conditions of any digital interactive media.

Article C7 – Marketing Communications and Children
This Code maintains that parents and/or guardians should be encouraged to participate in and/or supervise their children's interactive activities. Personal data concerning children should not be disclosed to third parties without the consent of the parents or guardians, as the case may be, or where disclosure is authorised by law. Children's data should not be disclosed by any third party. Any form of marketing publicity aimed at children should be appropriate and suitable for them.

Article C8 – Respecting Consumer Wishes
If a customer requests a marketeer or its company not to send any marketing communications to him/her, that request should be respected. In this connection, the Code draws the attention of marketeers to the General Provisions (Article 19 – data protection and privacy).

Article C9 – Respecting Consumer Use of Digital Interactive Media
Where other forms of digital marketing communications and/or application may allow consumers to open them, no interference should take place with the consumer's normal usage of or experience in digital interactive media.

Article C10 – Respect for the Potential Sensitivities of a Global Audience
Respect should be shown to the local (overseas) social norms and traditions and the principle of social responsibility contained in the General Provisions of this

Code should be adhered to given the extra national boundary reach of electronic networks.

Article C11 – Safety and Health
On this issue, the requirements embodied in Article A5 should be fulfilled by marketeers, as irresponsible practices in regard to this issue may endanger safety and health. Thus, not only products but also their samples should be suitably packaged for delivery to customers.

Article C12 – Right of Withdrawal
At the point of introducing a product, a marketeer should inform the prospective customer his/her right of withdrawal from the contract and identify the circumstances in which he/she should be allowed to do so.

Article C13 – After-Sales Service
In the event of offering after-sales service, the marketeer concerned should inform the customer of the details of this service, and the procedure for activating this service.

Article C14 – Prices and Credit Terms
If credit is offered by a marketeer, then the consumer should be provided with all the information in order to enable him/her to understand the cost, interest or any other conditions or terms attached to the deal. Similar obligations a marketeer should perform if the payment is allowed in instalments. In this context, the terms of payment will be different from those usually asked for products.

Article C15 – Unsolicited Products
A product, for which payment is expected, should only be delivered if it has a corresponding order. This provision should be read with the General Provisions (Article 21).

Article C16 – Fulfilment of Orders
According to this Code, unless otherwise stated in the offer, orders should be fulfilled within 30 working days after the order has been formally received from the prospective customer. Customers should be informed of any delay in the supplying of the product as soon as possible; any cancellations should be approved, and deposits, if relevant, should be given back immediately.

Article C17 – Substitution of Products
If a seller is unable to provide a product due to it not being available in the market and substitute or alternative product is supplied, if it is disliked by the consumer, then the latter should have the recourse to return the substitute or alternative product at the seller's expense.

Article C18 – Return of Faulty or Damaged Products
In the event of a consumer informing the marketeer that he/she has received a faulty or damaged product, it is the responsibility of the latter to bear the costs of returning the product(s).

Article C19 – Payment and Debt Collection
This is about collecting debts from consumers who have failed to make the agreed payments Article C19 asks the companies and direct sellers to be sympathetic in their approach when trying to collect lapsed payments.

Article C20 – Responsibility
Responsibility for all aspects of direct marketing and digital marketing activities lies with the seller/marketeer. In this connection, the user of this Code should refer to Article 23 of the General Provisions embodied in this Code. All parties involved in whatever capacity in direct or digital marketing should discharge their respective responsibilities identified in this Code.

This Code has made special provisions for telemarketing, a full discussion of which would be a bit irrelevant to the theme of this work as most of the rural areas in the majority of developing countries do not have the privilege of using telemarketing facilities. If, however, a marketeer or a consumer wishes to familiarise himself/herself with the Code-based provisions of telemarketing, he/she may like to refer to the relevant provisions of this Code (Article 21) – only a brief discussion of these provisions would seem to be appropriate.

Whereas *Article C21* defined certain important terms relating to telemarketing, namely, telemarketer, telemarketing, automatic dialling-announcing device and predictive dialling device, the remaining parts of the Article C21.1 – C21.6 deal with Disclosure of certain information, namely, the name of the marketeer; the purpose of the call; the identity number of the company that is calling; the main characteristics of the product; the terms and conditions of the contract and whether the prospective customer has understood them or not; the price of the product; the payment system and the manner of delivery of the product; the customer's rights, namely, the right of withdrawal from the contract; the terms of returning the goods when they may not be useful for the customer. Sellers should make outgoing calls only during hours deemed to be reasonable in the authority/ jurisdiction concerned; where an order is being placed, the consumer should receive confirmation in writing or by any other strong method, and it should contain the terms of the contract, including the requirements for withdrawal, if necessary; the date(s) of the delivery and other relevant information. Conversations between a marketeer and a prospective customer may be recorded but must be exclusively used for telemarketing purposes; such conversations, with the permission of the prospective customer may be used for training purposes and for the purposes of quality control. Consent must be sought from the participants before any recorded conversation is presented to a public audience.

If a consumer does not have a listed telephone number, he or she should not be contacted unless the prospective consumer himself/herself has disclosed his/her number to the marketeer.

Paragraph C21.6 is concerned with the use of predictive dialling services and automatic dialling answering services, which, given the current state of development in the majority of developing countries, particularly in rural areas, would be a rather pre-mature discussion of this issue. People in rural areas need to be familiar with an effective use of a very sophisticated type of technological device.

Article C22 – Interest-Based Advertising (IBA)
This article is worried about the way the sellers collect information over a period of time on how users use online to look at products and services. In other words, these are unsolicited publicity with a view to extending the customer base. Obviously, any technology-based operation needs to adopt certain precautionary measures. This Code therefore enters cautions to the prospective users of technology-based advertisements, including cautions that parents of children should be mindful of the adverse effect of this form of publicity for products.

8.6 Environmental Issues

8.6.1 Chapter D – Environmental Issues

Chapter D of the Code which is about environmental claims should be read with the 'General Provisions and Definitions on Advertising and Marketing Communications'.[6] ICC Framework for Responsible Environment Marketing Communications provides more information for marketeers interested in environmental claims.

As far as this Chapter is concerned, it relates to all marketing communications containing environmental claims in which direct or indirect reference may be made to environmental or ecological aspects relating to production, packaging, distribution, use/consumption or disposal of products. This Chapter has been developed over 7 (seven) Articles which have been briefly discussed below.

Article D1 – Honest and Truthful Presentation
It would not be difficult for any informed reader to anticipate the contents of this Article; nevertheless, the marketeer is the best person to know whether he/she has presented the products truthfully or not. Furthermore, they should be conversant with what provides protection to the environment and what does not. However, the main thrust of Article D1 is to ensure that marketeers perform their functions honestly and truthfully. That their products are environmentally friendly should be supported by evidence rather than taking advantage of the less-informed prospective customers particularly in rural areas. In fact, where a marketeer is not certain of whether his/her product is ecologically safe or sustainable, he/she

---

[6]https://2go.iccwbo.org/icc-consolidated-code-of-advertising-and-marketing-2011-english.html

should say so rather than providing a misleading information to the prospective consumer in regard to this issue. In fact, the deficiencies and advantages to their products with comparable products, if available, on the market, should be clearly identified and explained to a prospective customer. The prospective customers should also be informed of the sources where more information on the product may be available.

Article D2 – Scientific Research
Any kind of environmental terminology should be avoided where possible in any marketing communications, and instead the meaning of them should be explained in simple language to prospective customers. Proper evidence must be there to support publicity on any kind of benefit such as environmental claims relating to health and safety.

Article D3 – Superiority and Comparative Claims
Any claim which is deemed to be comparative should be specific and the basis for the comparison should be clear. This issue becomes important when two products in question, share almost similar attributes, and should also meet similar needs.

A marketeer should make it clear in a simple language whether the comparison is between its previous product and the current one, or between the product of a competitor and its own improved product. Improvement of the quality of a product and that of packaging are to be treated differently; thus, presentation of an improved product and that of an improved packaging must be kept separate, and a marketeer must identify primarily the reasons why the current product should be treated as an improved one. Packaging often simply makes a product more attractive; it does not contribute to the quality of a product.

Article D4 – Product Life cycle, Components and Elements
Environmental claims may not be confused with the stages of a product's life cycle; a marketeer should clearly explain to a prospective customer which stage of a product's life cycle or which property a claim refers to. The benefits of a life cycle claim should be substantiated by a life cycle analysis.

When a claim may refer to the reduction of elements which contributes to an environmental impact, it should be clearly explained what element(s) has/have actually been reduced and a claim may be justified only if it relates to 'components or elements which usually result in significant environmental improvement'. Thus, marketing advertiser should not make environmental claims if there is no association of it with the product being advertised. Similarly, the product should not be described in a way that it appears to have remarkable features unless such uniqueness can be supported by evidence.[7]

A marketing advertiser should be certain by possessing reliable scientific evidence to support an implied or express health and safety claim in compliance with the other relevant provisions of the Code.

---

[7]See further p. 41 of the Code.

Article D5 – Signs and Symbols
Environmental signs and symbols should only be used in marketing communications if the source of these signs and symbols are not confusing and have received a genuine approval of a certification authority.

Article D6 – Waste Handling
Environmental waste collection, processing and disposal methods would be satisfactory provided it is accepted by and available to the consumers, in general, or it is governed by the local law.

Article D7 – Responsibility
The Code reminded the readers that 'the rules on responsibility laid down in the General Provisions (Article 23) shall apply' to this Chapter. Furthermore, for additional guidance on environmental marketing communications an interested party may also like to consult the ICC Framework fort Responsible Environmental Marketing Communications, which is available on https://iccwbo.org/publication/icc-advertising-and-marketing-communications-code/

8.7 Conclusions

The Codes issued by the International Chamber of Commerce in 2018 are much more elaborate and indeed more instructive than the previous ones which have also been discussed in this work. One of the reasons for discussing the older version of the Code is to offer alternatives to deep rural people to initially follow the old ones unless they are capable of following the 2018 version of the Code. The rural people may find it useful to follow the previous Code published by the ICC; however, if they are already technologically advanced in certain rural areas in the developing world, they may be capable of coping with the demands of the 2018 Codes of Conduct which are, as stated above, more comprehensive and instructive than the former Codes of Conduct on marketing and advertising of products.

Over the years, the Western world, in general, has been very conscious of the rights of consumers, rather than the rights of sellers. In England, for example, the days of *caveat emptor* (buyer beware) are over, and there is no reason why a similar practice may not be adopted by the developing world, in particular, in their rural areas, rather than keeping them less informed of their rights as consumers. It is appreciated that the developing world, in general, lacks enforcement facilities, and upgrading of these facilities would take time and funds. There is no reason therefore why Codes of Conduct may not be implemented instead, and the local judiciaries combined with their local Chambers of Commerce take cognisance of the importance of these Codes of Conduct and treat them as binding instruments. This transformation of the system should be as effective as legislative instruments. Furthermore, what may be described as a 'high level of consumer rights awareness' would be created by implementing these Codes of Conduct; indeed, these Codes of Conduct have also educative value.

Chapter 9

Development and the Issue of the Protection and Preservation of the Environment

Abstract

The protection and preservation of the environment, whether of an urban area or a rural area may not be disregarded. Most of the rural areas in the world lacks the knowledge on this issue. In so far as the developing countries are concerned, it has now become a societal problem mainly owing to the lack of public awareness in the rural areas of these countries. This chapter examines the principal causes of the lack of public awareness. The author also examines the correlation between poverty and deterioration of the environment and between industrialisation and deterioration of the environment, where possible. Both sophisticated and unsophisticated technology cause pollution. The other causes of pollution, industrial or otherwise have also been identified and explained. The relevant UN Resolution, namely, the Permanent Sovereignty over Natural Resources 1962, the Charter of Economic Rights and Duties of States 1974, the UN World Commission on Environment and Development: Our Common Future (The Brundtland Report) have also received attention. The 17 Sustainable Development Goals have been mentioned.

In the opinion of the author, almost all of the important and relevant documents have received attention in this chapter in order to create awareness of the problems in connection with the protection of the environment.

Keywords: Public awareness; unguarded; uncovered construction; correlation; poverty

9.1 Introduction

The importance of the protection and preservation of the environment in the developing countries, in general, and the rural areas therein, cannot be ignored. A very large number of them are lagging behind industrial development. This is

Rural Marketing as a Tool for National Development, 133–152

Copyright © 2024 Charles Chatterjee

Published under exclusive licence by Emerald Publishing Limited

doi:10.1108/978-1-83608-064-020241010

primarily owing to the fact that the people living in the rural areas, in general, lack the requisite knowledge on this issue.

The lack of knowledge in the poor communities in the rural areas of developing countries may not necessarily be the effect of their fault; it is rather a societal problem which becomes manifest in the lack of their public awareness too. Therefore, public awareness should be developed at two levels with two different methods: (a) the general form of public awareness (societal public awareness) may be attempted to be developed primarily by means of publicities whether through posters, television or radio programmes with actual pictures of environmental damages, (b) the method of developing public awareness for the general public should primarily be imparted through capacity building sessions, but can also benefit from other means which have been suggested for attempting to develop public awareness at a societal level. The reader is reminded of the fact that the following discussion solely relates to the rural areas, in general, in developing countries.

9.2 Examining Some of the Principal Causes of the Lack of Public Awareness of People in the Rural Areas in the Developing Countries

It may be pointed out at the outset that the lack of public awareness in rural areas may also be found in the Western world although due to publicity given through the media, a rather minority of them may still lack the desired level of public awareness. Returning to the issue of the lack of public awareness of the people in the rural areas of the developing countries, the following seem to be the main causes of their lack of knowledge in regard to the protection and preservation of the environment:

- the societal habits of doing daily work relating to washing of clothes, cleaning cutleries, method of cooking, etc. traditionally in the rural areas without thinking and realising the adverse effect of their activities on the environment;
- making of large fires with logs particularly during the winter period, which causes significant amount of smoke;
- cooking in log fires in the open air pollutes the environment;
- burning of logs and wastes in the open, which causes smoke, is a very common phenomenon in the rural areas;
- observance of religious festivals in which large fires are often used, causing smoke;
- unguarded and uncovered construction works pollutes the environment;
- most of the roads in rural areas being unmetalled, any passing vehicle will pollute the environment; additionally, pollution is also created by petrol- or diesel-driven vehicles;
- in most of the rural areas, sewage systems, if at all exist, directly contribute to the pollution process of the environment;

- unregulated and consequently uncontrolled use of fertilisers in the agricultural fields would be a direct cause of pollution of the environment; and
- uncontrolled ways of fly-tipping or dumping rubbish, excess food or other non-usable stuff are the other ways of polluting the environment.

9.3 The Correlation Between Poverty and Deterioration of the Environment and Between Industrialisation and Deterioration of the Environment

The term 'poverty' need not be defined or explained. Both poverty and industrialisation process may be responsible for polluting the environment in two different ways, which are obvious. Thus, in terms of their activities against keeping the environment clean, both are guilty but the extent of the nature of their activities are different. The principal causes of poverty are manifold, namely, the lack of money for the family and its consequential effect; the lack of education, hence the lack of public awareness, and of course, the lack of capacity to develop any new ideas to build something useful for the country, such as in the agriculture and cottage industry sectors. Certain of the so-called developing countries, namely, China and India have developed quite a sophisticated form of agriculture; indeed, they are currently able to export very high-quality agricultural products abroad, and these products also meet the high standards prescribed by the Western world. Leather, copper (India) and of course IT, and China is described by many as the workshop of the entire world. Therefore, one may re-affirm that if a government has a policy to develop something it can happen. But, unfortunately, as stated earlier, that the majority of the governments in the developing world seem to be reluctant to developing their rural areas.

On the other hand, both sophisticated and unsophisticated technology cause pollution – one in a sophisticated and the other in an unsophisticated way – but the end result is the same. In this regard, the practice of developed and developing countries seems to be the same. In both types of country, the urban areas are more polluted than the rural areas.

Whereas the countries in the developed world have joined the race of industrialisation with all its merits and disadvantages, developing countries may like to do it sensibly, perhaps after a concerted international pollution prevention policy and the mechanism has been in place, and every country, rich or poor, would be obliged to follow them. The caution should be entered however that prior to developing any policy and legislation on this issue, every government should ensure that each of them will have sufficient enforcement officers with appropriate training in relation to this issue.

In many of the industrialised developed countries, there exists a practice whereby motor vehicles of any type would not be allowed to drive after they have attained a certain age. These countries have also restrictions on diesel and petrol-driven motor vehicles. It is appreciated that developing countries will take a rather long time to change over from their traditional practice on this over to an environment-friendly policy and system, nevertheless, they will be required to do so. Incidentally, the vast majority of the developing countries are tropical countries; there is no reason why over a period of time they may not be able to exploit solar energy rather than the traditional forms of energy, where possible. Many of the developed countries have already developed this system or are in the process of doing so.

Poverty in developing countries has become a part of the way of life of the people therein; there is no need to continue with this practice. It is an issue which has to be resolved by the indigenous people for the reasons explained in the chapter on Development in this work.

Industrialised countries do have poverty, but only up to a tolerable level, whereas poverty in the developing countries is not only a common phenomenon, but in almost all cases, it has far exceeded the tolerable level. Poverty has a demoralising effect on human beings, and it is one of the most important causes of migration of people from developing countries to developed countries aspiring a better life. All this would prove to be unnecessary if developing countries had adopted a people-centred approach to development, which would also be environmentally-friendly. On the other hand, too much industrialisation based on ill thought-out policies in many developed countries will be an environmentally unfriendly act, and also would cause cross-border pollution.

Incidentally, the Brundtland Report (then the Norwegian Prime Minister Mr Gro Harlem Brundtland) condemned uncontrolled and irresponsible industrialisation primarily owing to its adverse environmental impact on this planet.[1] This presents a dilemma; however, an international consensus on this issue is urgently needed and it has received further attention in a separate section of this chapter.[2]

The developing countries' right to explore and exploit their natural resources which are necessary for themselves, and foreign countries alike were confirmed by the UN General Assembly Resolution entitled Permanent Sovereignty over Natural Resources 1962, but it failed to see the possibilities of any over-exploitation of these resources and its adverse consequential effect on the international community. Of course, it must be accepted that the protection and preservation of the environment was not thought to be an important item in relation to private foreign investments during the 1960s; it appeared in the International Convention on the Law of the Sea Convention 1982 by which time international awareness on this issue was developed. It is to be emphasised, however, that it was the developing countries, in general, which actually took the initiative to demonstrate that they were equally concerned with the damages that pollution of the environment may cause; see for example, The Charter of Economic Rights and Duties of States 1974.[3] Then, of course, a number of examples of the international initiatives in the form of Conventions, Resolutions and Agreements have been developed, which have received attention in subsequent section of this work. It is to be emphasised that some of the developed

[1]This Report was published by the World Commission on The Environment and Development (WCED) sponsored by the UN and published in 1987.
[2]See 9.4.
[3]See paragraph (f) in the Preamble to the Charter and Article 29 and 30, in particular, of it.

industrialised countries are, it seems, really not so interested in controlling pollution caused by their industrial equipment or machines.

What is really needed, and needed urgently, is a consensus amongst the industrialised countries on the issue of pollution control, as otherwise, it will not only adversely affect the human and animal health but also the developing countries to a similar extent through cross-border pollution.

9.4 A Brief Examination of the Concept of Sustainable Development

Its literal meaning would signify that only 'development' will not do, it must be 'sustainable' too. The concept of 'sustainable' development became popular during the 1970s when the international community began registering their apprehension as to the environmental damage that might be caused to the planet. As explained, before that contrary to the popular belief, developing countries have, in general, shown their high degree of appreciation which led to the conclusion of some very meaningful documents some of which have already been referred to in the previous section of this work.

However, one should perhaps understand the literal meaning of the term 'sustainable'; it would simply mean something which may be 'sustained'. In 1987, the UN World Commission on *Environment and Development: Our Common Future*, otherwise known as the *Brundtland Report* defined 'sustainable development' as[4]

> ... development that meets the needs of the present without compromising the ability of the future generations to meet their own needs.

The term 'sustainable' according to the Cambridge Dictionary is

> Able to continue at the same level for a period of time.

> ... Causing little or no damage to the environment and therefore able to continue for a long time.[5]

Whereas the Shorter Oxford English Dictionary defined the term 'sustainable' as:

> Supportable, bearable; able to be upheld or defended.

> To sustain would mean cause to continue in a certain state, maintain at the proper level or standard.[6]

---

[4]See further UN General Assembly Document A/42/427 (www.un.org).
[5]The UN World Commission on Environment and Development (1987), popularly known as the Brundtland Report defined the term as '... development that meets the needs of the present without compromising the ability of future generations to meet their own needs'.
[6]Oxford, Oxford University Press (2007), vol I at 845.

The definition of the term 'sustainable' devised by Brundtland should not be construed to be wrong; it simply relates mainly to uneven development, poverty and population growth.

Incidentally, the first UN Conference on the Human Environment was held in Stockholm (Sweden) in 1972, the principal themes of it were[7]:

- to identify the interdependence between humankind and the natural environment;
- to emphasise the need for a global policy in regard to environmental issues; and
- to stress the connection between socio-economic development and the protection and preservation of the environment.

A comprehensive set of documents containing agreements of the Member of the UN principally on the issue of sustainable development was adopted by a very large number of States and which was formally accepted at the UN Conference on Environment and Development in 1992 (held in Rio de Janeiro). It was also then that the UN set up a Special Commission on Sustainable Development with the duty to monitor and report on the implementation of the Rio Declaration. In 2013, however, this Commission was replaced by the UN High Level Political Forum on Sustainable Development, which is working on negotiated declarations as well as for defining the 'development' agenda of the UN.

In so far as the UN is concerned it has already used its platform to create public awareness in regard to the need for the protection and preservation of the environment, and in particular, the interdependence of human beings and the natural environment in addition to highlighting the connection between socio-economic development and protection and preservation of the environment; however, the unanswerable question still remains whether a very large number of developing States may actually implement the provisions, for example, of the Rio Declaration of 1992; it was primarily an act of the developing countries.

Furthermore, the term 'sustainable development' still provokes controversy. What does it really mean for the ordinary people? The Millennium Goals also failed to implement its goals by 2015.[8] In 2015, the UN adopted a comprehensive document known as Sustainable Development Goals (which are 17 in number); its main objectives are to eradicate poverty, to develop environmental awareness and to ensure prosperity for all, over the next 15 years.[9] These goals are part of the UN's Sustainable Development Agenda.[10]

The following represents a brief account of the 17 sustainable development goals; but not all of them relate to rural development. Basically, it is the duty of

---

[7]https://www.un.org/en/conferences/environment/stockholm1972
[8]See, for example, M Jacob, 'Toward a Methodological Critique of Sustainable Development', 28 *Journal of Developing Areas* (1994) at 237–252.
[9]https://unric.org/en/wp-content/uploads/sites/15/2020/01/sdgs-eng.pdf.
[10]See the Resolution adopted by the UN General Assembly on 25 September 2015; Ref A/Res/70/1.

each of the governments of developing States to formulate their own rural policies – an issue of the domestic sovereignty.

(1) To end poverty in all its forms everywhere;
(2) To end hunger, achieve food security and improved nutrition and promote sustainable agriculture;
(3) To ensure healthy lives and promote well-being for all ages;
(4) To ensure gender equality education and promote lifelong learning opportunities for all;
(5) To achieve gender equality and empower all women and girls;
(6) To ensure availability and sustainable management of water and sanitation for all;
(7) To ensure access to affordable, reliable, sustainable and modern energy for all;
(8) To promote sustained, inclusive and sustainable economic growth, full and productive employment and decent work for all;
(9) To build resilient infrastructure, promote inclusive and sustainable industrialisation and foster innovation;
(10) To reduce inequality within and among countries;
(11) To make cities and human settlements inclusive, safe, resilient and sustainable;
(12) To ensure sustainable and production patterns;
(13) To take urgent action to combat climate change and its impacts;
(14) To conserve and sustainably use the oceans, seas and marine reserves for sustainable development;
(15) To protect, restore and promote sustainable use of terrestrial ecosystems, sustainably managed forests, combat desertification, and halt and reverse land degradation and biodiversity loss;
(16) To promote peaceful and inclusive societies for sustainable development, provide access to justice for all and build effective, accountable and inclusive institutions at all levels; and
(17) To strengthen the means of implementation and revitalise the global partnership for sustainable development.

But for the word, 'To', every single goal has been quoted from the UNGA Resolution *ad verbatim*. Interestingly enough, except for a limited number of goals, namely those at 14, 16 and 17, most of the other goals are directly or partially or indirectly relevant to the very theme of this work. By virtue of the goals being self-explanatory, there is no need to go into any details of them. Nevertheless, it would be appropriate to summarise a few of these goals to appropriately emphasise them and relate them once again to the principal themes of this work.

Briefly, it has been stated before that irrespective of whether national governments are able to adopt rural policies and provide finance to effectuate them, poverty particularly in the rural areas, both closer and distant areas from the urban areas, are urgently required to be ended in all its forms in a constructive way. The most effective way of dealing with rural poverty, in general, is to provide opportunities to rural people to earn money; this may be done by providing them training in capacity building which has been discussed in a good detail in this work.

After acquiring the minimum knowledge in a profession, in addition to some good knowledge in the language for a meaningful communication ability, the rural people irrespective of their gender, may find it convenient to work initially for their own small industries and the agriculture sector, which is the most important sector of all in all countries. This sector can create a significant number of employment too.

Each item of the Sustainable Development Goals has been systematically divided into various sub-items, and there is hardly any point in going into the details of each of the sub-paragraphs under the main goals.

The sources of poverty are manifold: the lack of education, the lack of proficiency in any discipline and no savings so as to be able to set up small businesses. But most of these deficiencies in human beings may be overcome through basic education and/or training – capacity building. Agriculture happens to be the largest sector in most of the developing countries, and already in many countries this sector of the economy is partly if not fully mechanised. High-quality agricultural products will have export markets too; especially by virtue of being low cost of production it has usually been possible for developing countries to find export markets for their agricultural products. This is a sector of opportunities, but from a financial standpoint, it usually increases dependency of the rural areas upon their central or state governments unless, of course, the local community takes the initiative to raise the necessary funds; of course, the second choice is better than the first.

If the first goal is successfully implemented, the second, the third and the fourth etc should necessarily ensue.

In the discussion of capacity-building, the issues of gender equality (Goal 5), and the need for capacity-building in order to ensure availability and management of water and sanitation for all (Goal 6) have been referred to.

The subject matter of Goal 7 – to ensure access to affordable, reliable, sustainable and modern energy for all – is very much a matter for the central and state governments; however, with sufficient capacity building in solar energy, in particular, rural areas should conform to this goal. It is maintained that the rural areas would need financial help from their own governments on this issue.

There is no reason why the subject-matter of Goal 8 – to promote sustained, inclusive and sustainable economic growth, full and productive employment and decent work for all – may not be achieved after the rural people have volunteered to earn their knowledge and work capacity in various trade schemes and professions.

The subject matter of Goal 9 – *build resilient infrastructure, promote inclusive and sustainable industrialisation and foster innovation* – is primarily meant for the urban areas in a developing country; but there is no reason why rural areas may not be utilised, with appropriate training of the people therein, as a hinterland for providing materials for those industries.

Goal 10, the objective of which is to reduce inequality within and among countries, is achievable through lessons against prejudices, but it may be found very difficult to achieve. Prejudice against people, between men and women and between different complexions and origins are very common even within many Western States too. In the United Kingdom, a large number of legislations to abolish inequality exist and yet, a very large number of litigation on this issue are referred particularly to Employment Tribunals every year.[11]

Goal 11, the objective of which is to make cities and human settlements inclusive, safe, resilient and sustainable, is primarily a task for the government of a State to perform. However, with an increase in employment in the rural areas of a State, people in those areas should be able to achieve this objective in their areas too provided, of course, they create good facilities for general use.

Goal 12 which aims to ensure sustainable consumption and production patterns is primarily a matter for the entire world. This Goal is not only concerned with sustainable consumption and production, but also with the issue of 'environmentally sound management of chemicals and all wastes throughout their life cycle, in accordance with agreed international frameworks, and significantly reduce their release to air, water and soil in order to minimise their adverse impacts on human health'.[12] This is where capacity-building sessions at both urban and rural areas in a country become extremely relevant. In the rural areas in a country, in particular, majority of the people living there, are not familiar with those issues, and many of them are not aware at all of the adverse effect of the unacceptable use of wastes and water, whether in ponds or rivers or canals etc.

Goal 13 – to take urgent action to combat climate change and its impacts – on this issue, one should be familiar with the UN Framework Convention on Climate Change, and it is for the central governments, in both rich and poor countries, UN and its relevant agencies, namely UNEP (the UN Environmental Programme) in Nairobi, WTO, WHO etc, and the entire international community along with the relevant NGOs, INGOs and various regional bodies to reach consensus on how best to implement the provisions of the UN Framework Convention in both developed and developing countries.

Goal 14 – to conserve and sustainably use the oceans, seas and marine resources for sustainable development – the primary issues of this goal have also been included in UNCLOS III (UN Convention on the Law of the Sea, 1982) which provides '... legal framework for the conservation and sustainable use of oceans and their resources' Usually, breaches of any of the Convention provisions are referred to the Sea Tribunals.[13]

Whereas Goal 15 is primarily concerned with environmental issues embracing the entire world, the main objective of Goal 16 is to 'promote peaceful and inclusive societies for sustainable development, provide access to justice for all and build effective, accountable and inclusive institutions at all levels'. These two

---

[11]Official data change every year.
[12]Stated in paragraph 12.4 of the Goal 12.
[13]See sub-paragraph 14c of Goal 14.

objectives are ideally to reach decisions on unresolved issues by the international community.

By the same token, the objectives of Goal 17, to 'strengthen the means of implementation and revitalise the global partnership for sustainable development', is another issue which needs international cooperation to develop guidelines which, given the nature of the States' attitudes, is believed that it may encounter many difficulties; but one can only hope for the best. If, however, any world-wide consensus is attained, the rural areas of each State will be obliged to enforce them, and as a consequence these areas will benefit from an effective enforcement of this consensus.

Nevertheless, one has to appreciate that the UN Framework Convention on Climate Change is a step forward; however, the target date for implementing all these Goals is 2030. A brief account of the nature of the international action for the protection and preservation of the environment would be very relevant to the rural population too.

9.5 A Brief Critical Analysis of Some of the Instruments Concluded by the International Community with a View to Raising Public Awareness

First, initiative taken by the United Nations was translated into the *Stockholm Declaration* (1972) which was adopted by the UN Conference on Human Environment of 16 June 1972, but some of its provisions were objected to by a number of developing countries, and in particular, Principle 20 of the Draft Declaration which was prepared by the Preparatory Committee on the grounds that the proposed obligation to consult developing States might be derogated by many of the developed States to slow down development projects.[14]

Paragraph 6 of the Preamble to the Declaration stated, inter alia, that:

> A point has been reached in history when we must shape our actions throughout the world with a more prudent care for their environmental consequences. Through ignorance or indifference, we can do massive and irreversible harm to the earthly environment on which our life and well-being depend.

Principle 6 of the Declaration, for example, stated, inter alia, that:

> The discharge of toxic substances or of other substances and the release of heat, in such quantities or concentrations as to exceed the capacity of the environment to render them harmless, must be halted in order to ensure that serious or irreversible damage is not inflicted upon ecosystems.

---

[14]Op cit.

The environmental problems are too pronounced in the developing countries, in general; and as stated earlier that public awareness of the environmental problems, how these problems are created and the remedies thereof, is a perfect topic for capacity building in the population in rural areas.

Finally, Principle 26 of the Declaration provides that:

> Man, and his environment must be spared the effects of nuclear weapons and all other means of mass destruction. States must strive to reach prompt agreement, in the relevant international organs, for the elimination and complete destruction of such weapons.

Each of these Principles is fundamentally important for both urban and rural areas in a country. Each of these Principles is instructive and well thought-out.

Second, the *UN General Assembly Resolution 37/7 on a World Charter for Nature, 28 October 1982*.[15] This Resolution was adopted by 111 States in favour, 1 against (the United States) and with 18 abstentions. The principal objective of the Resolution was to offer guidelines to the Members of the United Nations in order to enable them to develop their domestic legislations along the lines suggested by this Resolution. Abstentions may happen when the States concerned, or a group of States, register their indifference to it, or according to them some of the provisions of a resolution, if not all, would run counter to their national interest – an insoluble problem based on a rigid sense of sovereignty maintained by many States.

In the Preamble to this Charter, it stated, inter alia, that:

> Recalling that, in its resolution 35/7 of 30 October 1980, it expressed its conviction that the benefits which could be obtained from nature depended on the maintenance of natural processes and on the diversity of life forms and that those benefits were jeopardised by the excessive exploitation and the destruction of natural habitats.

It further reminded the Member States of the United Nations that:

> ... in the exercise of their permanent sovereignty over their natural resources, to conduct their activities in recognition of the supreme importance of protecting natural systems, maintaining the balance and quality of nature and conserving natural resources, in the interest of present and future generations.[16]

---

[15]https://digitallibrary.un.org/record/39295
[16]See further UNGA Resolution 1803 of 1962 entitled Permanent Sovereignty over Natural Resources.

The Preamble further states that:

> Lasting benefits from nature depend upon the maintenance of essential ecological processes and life support systems, and upon the diversity of life forms, which are jeopardised through essential exploitation and habitat destruction by man.

The World Charter of Nature consists of 24 Articles over three headings: (a) General Principles; (b) Functions; and (c) Implementation. In the context of this work, it is felt that there is no need to go into any details of the above three items.[17]

Third, the *UN Framework Convention on Climate Change of 9 May 1992*.[18] This Framework Convention was accepted by almost all the Member States of the UN. It came into force on 21 March 1994, and it consists of 24 Articles; furthermore, no reservations would be made to the Convention, simply because it is a framework Convention the sole purpose of which was to provide guidelines as to how the Members of the UN should develop their legislation on climate change.

Article 2 of the Convention provides the ultimate objective of it:

> The ultimate objective of this Convention and any related legal instruments that the Conference of the Parties may adopt it to achieve, in accordance with the relevant provisions of the Convention, stabilisation of greenhouse gas concentrations in the atmosphere at a level that would prevent dangerous anthropogenic interference with the climate system.[19] Such a level should be achieved within a time-frame sufficient to allow ecosystems to adapt naturally to climate change, to ensure that food production is not threatened and to enable economic development to proceed in a sustainable manner.

Upon an analysis of the above provision, it would appear that one of its objectives is to achieve 'stabilisation of greenhouse gas concentrations in the atmosphere at a level that would prevent dangerous anthropogenic interference with the climate system'.

According to this Framework Convention, 'climate change':

> ... means a change of climate which is attributed directly or indirectly to human activity that alters the composition of the global atmosphere and which is in addition to natural climate variability observed over comparable time periods.

---

[17]Op cit.

[18]https://unfccc.int/resource/docs/convkp/conveng.pdf.

[19]It means, pertaining to anthropogeny: the investigation of the origin of humans; see further *The Shorter Oxford English Dictionary*, Oxford, Oxford University Press (2007) at 90.

'Climate change' may therefore be attributed directly or indirectly to *human activity*, as it often alters the composition of the global atmosphere.[20] The Framework Convention thus places emphasis upon the adverse dimensions to 'irresponsible human activities' which should be prevented by governmental legislation and the corresponding enforcement measures by informed enforcement officers. Here is again the importance of providing 'capacity building' lessons to both urban and rural population.

At this point, it would be appropriate to refer to the definitions of certain core terms provided by the Convention. According to this Convention, 'climate system' would mean:

> ... the totality of the atmosphere, hydrosphere, bio-sphere, geosphere and their interactions.

'Greenhouse gases' means:

> those gaseous constituents of the atmosphere, both natural and anthropogenic, that absorb and re-emit infrared radiation.[21]

'Reservoir' means:

> ... a component or components of the climate system where a greenhouse gas or a precursor of a greenhouse gas is stored.

'Sink' would mean:

> ... any process, activity or mechanism which removes a greenhouse gas, an aerosol or a precursor of a greenhouse gas from the atmosphere.

Source means:

> ... any process or activity which releases a greenhouse gas, an aerosol or a precursor of a greenhouse gas into the atmosphere.

It would now be appropriate to state briefly the attempts made by the United Nations on the issue of climate change and an urgent need for protecting and preserving the environment were numerous; and many of those attempts preceded the Framework Convention; for example, the UN General Assembly Resolution 44/228 of 22 December 1989 on the UN Conference on Environment and Development and resolutions 43/53 of 6 December 1988, 44/207 of 22 December 1989, 45/212 of 21 December 1990 and 46/169 of 19 December 1991 on Protection of Global Climate for

---

[20]Emphasis added.
[21]Means electromagnetic radiations.

Present and Future Generations of Mankind. Reference should also be made to UNGA Res 44/206 of 22 December 1989 on the possible adverse effect of sea-level rise on island and coastal areas and the relevant provisions of UNGA Res 44/172 of 19 December 1989 on the implementation of the Plan of Action to Combat Desertification. One should also refer to the Vienna Convention for the Protection of the Ozone Layer, 1985, and the Montreal Protocol on Substances that Deplete the Ozone Layer, 1989, as adjusted and amended on 29 June 1990; the Ministerial Declaration of the Second World Climate Conference adopted on 7 November 1990 and the relevant provisions of the Declaration of the United Nations Conference on the Human Environment, adopted at Stockholm on 16 June 1972.

Under the UN Framework Convention, the Parties to it are required to implement a number of commitments, and instead of quoting each of these commitments, it would be more appropriate to emphasise that the States are required to take urgent steps for protecting and preserving the environment. The most important starting point would be to raise the level of public awareness in both urban and rural areas of each State. It is appreciated that governments will have a difficult task to raise public awareness in the rural areas in their country, but nevertheless, it has to be achieved; the rural areas deserve more attention than the urban areas in a country, otherwise both the natural resources and the large human resources will remain unused.

Fourth, the *Rio Declaration on the Environment and Development of 16 June 1992*.[22] The Rio Declaration of 1992 was, in reality, adopted for furthering the theme of the Stockholm Declaration. One of the most important provisions of the Rio Declaration refers for payment of compensation by the polluter of the environment in any way which, in fact, is often described as the 'polluter pays principle' (Principle 13).

The Rio Declaration consists of 27 Principles and identified the bases upon which the States and peoples therein can co-operate and develop rules of international law on sustainable development.

However, in the context of climate change, there is little point in referring to each of the Principles of this Declaration; hence, only the Principles most relevant to this chapter have received attention.

Principle 2 of the Declaration provides that:

> States have, in accordance with the Charter of the United Nations and the principles of international law, the sovereign right to exploit their own resources pursuant to their own environmental and development policies, and the responsibility to ensure that activities within their jurisdiction or control do not cause damage to the environment of other States or areas beyond the limits of national jurisdiction.

---

[22]See *International Law Documents*, 13th edition, Oxford University Press (2017), at 7.

This Principle acknowledges that although on the one hand sovereign States have their sovereign right to exploit their own resources, they may not be allowed to cause any harm, including environmental damage, to their neighbours by causing what is usually known as 'transboundary pollution'.[23] However, unfortunately, this Principle failed to refer to the link between environmental damage and climate change, although in subsequent principles, if closely analysed, one may find an indirect reference to it.

This Principle also assumes that all developing States will have effective environmental and development policies with appropriately trained enforcement officers, which may not necessarily be the case, although from a theoretical standpoint, every State may produce its environmental and development policies; if it were so, then poor countries would not have remained poor nor would they have contributed to the polluting process of their environment and also the environment of the neighbouring countries.

By the same token, Principle 7 of the Declaration states that:

> States shall co-operate in a spirit of global partnership to conserve, protect, and restore the health and integrity of the Earth's ecosystem. In view of the different contributions to global environmental degradation, States have common but different responsibilities...

In theory, the provisions of this Principle are correct; however, global partnership on any issue would require a high degree of co-operation between States which hardly exists. Furthermore, in order to achieve 'global partnership' each partner will be required to share common ideas on any issue, which is again almost non-existent. However, the provisions of this Principle are correct.

Principle 13 provides that:

> States should develop national law regarding liability and compensation for the victims of pollution and other environmental damage. States shall also co-operate in an expeditious and more determined manner to develop further international law regarding liability and compensation for adverse effects of environmental damage caused by activities within their jurisdiction or controls to areas beyond their jurisdiction.

The use of the word 'should' in Principle 13 weakens the strength of the Principle, unless of course, it is maintained that based on the philosophy of the Rio Declaration, 'should' will have the force of 'shall'. It is a long-awaited provision, and Rio Declaration was very much a product initiated by the developing

---

[23]The first arbitration on this issue was held as early as 1938 and 194 (Trail Smelter Arbitrations) between the United States and Canada; see the Arbitration Reports in 3 R.I.A.A (1941) at 1905.

countries along with other countries. But perhaps the unanswerable question remains whether the large industries, both domestic and foreign, would minimise the pollution process at all by replacing their technology and/or using environmentally-friendly fuel. This is where a world-wide consensus is necessary. Unless it is a matter of 'international concern' it would be difficult for any State to control areas beyond its own jurisdiction. Bi-lateral negotiations leading to a mutually acceptable arrangement would be the best option in the circumstances. Principle 13 should be read with Principle 16 of the Declaration.

The provisions of Principles 24 and 25 may be extended to include climate change too. Principe 24 provides that:

> Warfare is inherently destructive of sustainable development. States shall therefore respect international law providing protection for the environment in times of armed conflict and co-operate in its further development.

Article 2 paragraph (4) of the UN Charter aims at prohibiting warfare. But quite a number of the Members of the UN are already in breach of their obligations on this issue, in consequence of which in addition to killing people and destroying their homes, they have also polluted the environment by using high technology in the warfare. Sadly, the international community has largely remained reticent on this issue and failed to take any prohibitive action through international co-operation.

Article 25 provides that:

> Peace, development and environmental protection are interdependent and indivisible.

The provision of this Article is absolutely true but perhaps the order of the items should have been different in order to show the progression between them. The order could have been:

> Environmental protection, development and peace are interdependent and indivisible.

Two apparent issues seem to have stood in its way to fulfilling the objective of Principle 25: (a) the lack of willingness on the part of industries to co-operate universally on the issue of keeping the environment clean, in addition to manufacturing products such as motor vehicles in a way which would be environmentally friendly and (b) the lack of creation of public awareness in both urban and rural areas.

9.6 Conclusions

In developing this chapter, attention has been paid to the issues which have been considered to be important to explain the causes of why progress in development in the developing world has been slow, and the chapter's sub-headings have been developed and examined accordingly. In addition to the lack of public awareness, this chapter has also paid attention to the issue that there does exist a correlation between poverty and deterioration of the environment and between industrialisation and deterioration of the environment, and that one of the effective means of dealing with this issue would be to raise the level of public awareness particularly in the rural areas in countries. But almost an un-resolvable problem is presented by the unrelenting activities in the name of industrialisation even though these activities directly pollute the environment. Of course, some of the Western countries are taking action against these activities, albeit rather slowly.

The chapter has also attempted to explain the concept of 'sustainable development' which is thought to be a difficult concept for many people. Then, of course, the chapter also held a brief examination of the nature of action the international community has planned to take with a view to raising the level of public awareness for understanding the close relationship that exists between the maintenance of a clean environment and climate change.

However, the road to reach a clear consensus on this issue seems to be bumpy. It should be emphasised that the primary purpose of this chapter is not to examine all the relevant instruments and/or international attempts made for reaching consensus on the issue of how binding agreements on the protection of the environment and climate change may be reached but to critically examine the level of public awareness with regard to the issue of the correlation between development and protection and preservation of the environment, in addition to examining briefly the relationship between deterioration of the environment for whatever reasons and climate change.

The remit of this work has already been identified; nevertheless, it is worth reminding the readers that most of the countries in the developing world seem to bear prejudices against the rural areas in them; for example, over-deforestation leads to desertification which, in turn, adversely affects the environment. But what prohibitive measures are taken by the central or state government of the country concerned? In fact, trees and plants consume carbon dioxide and supply oxygen, therefore, deforestation is culpable for the rise of carbon dioxide in the Earth's atmosphere.

Deforestation is believed to be the cause of certain diseases, namely, malaria, sand fly disease to name but a few. Transmission of deadly virus of malaria by mosquitoes is a very common cause of the disease in Africa and Asia. The pandemic on coronavirus disease also started in China. Deforestation aids the proliferation of this disease in these areas which help multiply the number of mosquitoes. Furthermore, the lack of sanitation at homes and in stagnant waters which are very common in developing countries, in particular, in their rural areas, also contribute to spreading these diseases, in consequence of which many people in their countries die every year. Improved housing in the rural areas with other related facilities might change this situation, in addition to raising public awareness of basic human health issues.

Deforestation also leads to warming temperatures in consequence of which the incidence of rainfall becomes low with its attendant consequences. Environmentalists, in general, maintain that deforestation very much contributed to climate change. Greenhouse gas also adds to the climate change process. Greenhouse gas emissions are contributed to by human activities, which may be controlled provided both large and small industrial corporations, the services of which are indispensable to societies, are subject to rigid legislation and enforcement measures. Furthermore, when an irrigation system is badly designed, that is, not up to the international standards, it would do more harm to agriculture than good; by the same token, over-irrigation can also cause harm to agricultural land.[24] In relation to irrigation it may be pointed out that either there is over-irrigation or irresponsible use of it. Some of the examples of the countries that over-exploit ground water for irrigation are Bangladesh, China, India, Pakistan and sub-Saharan Africa, in general. Such acts also cause far-reaching environmental damage to rivers in any country, even neighbouring countries.[25]

Examples of the causes of environmental damage and its consequential adverse effect on climate change seem to be almost never-ending. Instead of elongating this discussion, it may be stated that the need for responsible use of the environment and at the same time heighten the level of public awareness, particularly in the rural areas in States, are of paramount importance. At this point, as an attempt to conclude this chapter, a few examples of the efforts made by the international community may be briefly discussed.

The World Development Report of 2016 identified the complexity of the environmental issues. They are numerous, but most important issues have been referred to in this work. One of the outstanding contributions of this Report was that it considered economic growth as an integral part of environmental sustainability; indeed, this Report was preceded by the Sustainable Development Goals of 2015. So, one can easily see the connection between these two documents.

On the other hand, the Kyoto Protocol of 1998 could have been discussed immediately following the discussion of the UN Framework Convention, but it is no longer in force and has officially lost its importance as the Sustainable Development Goals of 2015 are supposed to be materialised by 2030. The order in terms of the dates of the instruments has otherwise been maintained.

By the same token, the Montreal Protocol on Substances that Deplete the Ozone Layer, 1987 which was subsequently adjusted and amended has not been discussed in this work as it was primarily concerned with the limitation or reduction of certain gases which are caused by aviation and marine bunker fuels.

Although the Kyoto Protocol is no longer in force, it nevertheless identified certain policies and measures which the Parties to the Protocol should implement. In consonance with the theme of this work, the Protocol provided, inter alia, the following:

- Enhancement of energy efficiency in relevant sectors of the national economy;
- Promotion of sustainable forms of agriculture in light of climate change considerations; and

---

[24]See further Helmut Geist, *The Causes and Progression of Desertification*, Aldershot, Ashgate Publishing (2005).

[25]See further J Shapiro, *China's Environmental Challenges*, 2nd edition. Cambridge (England), Polity Press.

- Limitation and/or reduction of methane emissions through recovery and use of waste management, as well as in the production, transport and distribution of energy.[26]

In the context of this work, the people in the rural areas in any country should be required to raise their awareness of these issues in relation to the agricultural sector of the economy.

Finally, the Paris Agreement which came into force on 4 November 2016 has now turned out to be largely an academic exercise. The Paris Agreement, which was adopted by 195 countries and was supposed to be a legally binding instrument did not turn out to be so. The fate of the Agreement was not only determined by the United States but also by some of the countries particularly in Asia, namely China and India. Whereas China was apprehensive of the prospects of too much monitoring of her domestic policies, India, on the other hand, demonstrated her fear that a binding agreement would restrict her economic growth – again, a display of a rigid sense of sovereignty in respect of their (China and India) domestic issues.

Unfortunately, neither climate change nor the environmental issues seem to have received any priority in the behaviour of many countries. The real answer seems to be that many of the countries relying upon their traditional sources of income, namely, oil, coal or other forms of natural resources, have not developed in any significant way the other sources of income as yet. If these countries do not shift their position from their traditional sources of income, futile international attempts at climate change and environmental pollution will also remain with us. Perhaps, one should motivate women in most areas to take the initiative to change the attitudes of the world of men, which by coincidence, is one of the principal themes of this work.[27]

The reasons for emphasising the need for strengthening the rural areas particularly in developing countries are manifold: (a) in developing countries the rural areas are, in general, poorer than their urban areas; (b) consequently, poverty becomes very evident in those areas; (c) there exist a close connection between poverty and the deterioration of the environment; and (d) in an attempt to avoid poverty and to find an enjoyable life poor people often migrate into their urban areas, but unfortunately, owing to the lack of education and/or training, the vast majority of them remain unemployed or settle down for very low-level employment.

---

[26]See Article 2(a), sub-paragraphs (i), (iii) and (viii) of the Protocol.

[27]See further UN Security Council Resolution 1325 on *Women, Peace and Security* (available online); see also D Glenwright, 'Ottawa's Focus on Aid Delivery for Women is Smart – and Will Save Money', *Globe and Mail*, 11 June 2017; M C Nussbaum, *Women and Human Development – The Capabilities Approach*, New York, Cambridge University Press; UNDP, *The Future We Want: Rights and Empowerment – UNDP Gender Equality Strategy* 2014–2017, New York, UNDP (2014); UNDP, *Human Development Report* 2016 – *Human Development for Everyone*, New York, UNDP; J H Momsen, *Gender and Development*, London (England), Routledge (2004); see also *The Convention on the Elimination of All Forms of Discrimination Against Women* 2015, New York, the UN Treaty Collection and *Human Development Indicators*, New York, UNDP (2015), Table 5.

It is appreciated that the task of rural development is an onerous one; however, if it is not achieved, its consequential effect will ensue. It has been emphasised that governments in developing countries should not increase their debt burden by borrowing from various external sources including international financial institutions and foreign governments. It has therefore been suggested that, in allowing foreign corporations for investment purposes, conditions may be entered into the bi-lateral investment agreements between the two governments concerned, whereby these corporations will be required to set up a few of their offices in the remote rural areas with a view to providing the people capacity building training in both the main sectors, agriculture and industry.

No work on socio-economic development would be complete unless certain other issues, namely, armed conflict, violence and their consequences on a development process, gender discrimination and its consequential effect on the society and its economy, migration and its effect on the economy etc are resolved. It is believed that rural development should be taken seriously as developed rural areas may form the platforms for urban development, in addition to developing human resources with its attendant advantages in the rural areas in a State.

Conclusions

The concept of 'development' has been developed by many authors from a theoretical perspective, even in an abstract discourse. Westernisation in the name of 'development' in developing countries has often become manifest in carrying out development work in those countries. Time has now arrived to reflect on the causes of failure to achieve 'development'. These causes are primarily of two types: (a) internal and (b) external. Internal causes are manifold – the lack of appropriate planning and strategies on the part of developing countries in general; the lack of democracy, culminating in the denial of the rights and freedoms of people, in consequence of which their voice and participation were denied; the lack of continuity of governmental policies; the perception of development was not differentiated from Westernisation; the lack of capacity building; the lack of policies in rural development, etc. In fact, the list of deficiencies would be very long; and the external causes would mainly consist of large amounts of foreign aid in the belief that financial aid would be the most important factor of development without being appreciated by developing countries, in general, that too much foreign aid not only increases the burden of debt but also increases dependency on the aid givers with their adverse consequential effects too; that most of the 'developers' lacked a thorough knowledge of the developing countries, and of course, most of them lacked experience in that kind of activity.

However, by living in history, one might not be able to proceed fast and constructively. It has been clearly stated in this work that development must be achieved by the indigenous people and by indigenous means. Human resources development, which entails, inter alia, education and skills development, health and related issues, seems to have been ignored by many developing countries.

Development does not dawn on any country overnight; it is a long-drawn process. Furthermore, it should be achieved by the indigenous people, including women, through a learning process. Foreign entities of whatever nature, when invited into a developing country, should be contractually required to build the capabilities of the host country's people by exchanging ideas between themselves. It does not require any additional 'aid', both parties would be involved in learning new things and passing on their knowledge to the other party.

Rural Marketing as a Tool for National Development, 153–154
Copyright © 2024 Charles Chatterjee
Published under exclusive licence by Emerald Publishing Limited
doi:10.1108/978-1-83608-064-020241011

Education, including training, is an essential component of development; it enlightens peoples' minds, creates new ideas and makes a country inventive and innovative. The important theme of this work has been that marketing in rural areas in a country can be a factor in development as it entails education and skills too. When people have attained education and skills, the development process will be participatory; it should also raise the level of public awareness and the socio-economic dimension of life.

Bibliography

Alexandre, C. (2010). *Policymakers create room for experiments with banking beyond branches.* Global Savings Forum, Bill and Melinda Gates Foundation.

Amin, S. (2003). *Obsolescent capitalism: Contemporary politic and global disorder.* Zed Books.

Arnold, S. (2018). Financial exclusion in Kenya: Examining the changing picture 2006–2009 in financial inclusion in Kenya. *Survey Results and Analysis from FinAccess,* 2009 (S Arnold et al) Chapter 5, Nairobi FSD Kenya and Central Bank of Kenya. https://www.fsdkenya.org/blogs-publications/publications/2018-annual-report/

Baran, P. N. (1957). *The political economy of growth.* Monthly Review Press.

Chaia, A., Dalal, A., Goland, T. Gonzalez, M. J., Morduch, J., & Schiff, R. (2009). *Half the world is unbanked, financial access initiative framing note.* Financial Access Institute.

Chambers, R. (1983). *Rural development: Putting the last first.* Prentice Hall.

Chatterjee, S. K. (1986). *International law of development. Encyclopaedia of Public International Law.* Max Planck Institute for Comparative Public Law and International Law.

Chatterjee, S. K. (1987). The convention establishing the multilateral investment guarantee agency. *International and Comparative Law Quarterly, 36,* 76–91.

Chatterjee, S. K. (1991).The charter of economic rights and duties of states: An evaluation after fifteen years. *International and comparative law quarterly, 40*(3), 669–684.

Chatterjee, S. K. (1992). Forty years of international action for trade liberalisation. *Journal of World Trade, 23,* 45.

Chatterjee, C. (1996a). *The reality of risks in private foreign investment.* International Company and Commercial Law Review.

Chatterjee, C. (1996b). *Legal aspects of transnational marketing and sales contracts.* Cavendish.

Chatterjee, C. E. (2002). *Commerce the law for business managers.* Financial World Publishing.

Chatterjee, C. (2006). *Legal aspects of trade finance.* Routledge.

Collier, P. (2008). *The bottom billion: Why the poorest countries are failing and what can be done about it.* Oxford University Press.

Cowen, M. P., & Shenton, R. W. (1996). *Doctrines of development.* Routledge.

Devitt, P. (1977). Notes on poverty-oriented rural development. In *Extension, planning and the poor, agricultural administration unit occasional paper.* Overseas Development Institute.

Eade, D. (1997/2007). *Capacity-building: An approach to people-centred development.* Oxfam.

Eade, D., & Williams, S. (1995–1999). *The oxfam handbook of development and relief.* https://archive.org/details/oxfamhandbookofd00debo

Easterly, W. (2013). *The tyranny of experts: Economists, dictators and the forgotten rights of the poor.* Basic Books.

Ferguson, N. (2013). *The great degeneration – How institutions decay and economics die.* Penguin Group.

Geist, H. (2005). *The causes and progression of desertification.* Routledge.

Glenwright, D. (2017, June 11). Ottawa's focus on aid delivery for women is smart and will save money. *The Globe and Mail.* https://www.theglobeandmail.com/opinion/ottawas-focus-on-aid-delivery-for-women-is-smart-and-will-save-money/article35269202/

Guigale, M. M. (2014). *Economic development: What everyone needs to know.* Oxford University Press.

Haqul, M. (1976). *The poverty curtain: Choices for the third world.* Columbia University Press.

Hayek, F. A. (2007). *The road to serfdom: Text and documents.* Bruce Caldwell (ed.), 1944. University of Chicago Press.

Hornbeck, S. K. (1909). The most-favoured Nation clause (Part I). *American Journal of International Law, 3,* 797–827.

International Law Documents (13th ed.). (2017). Oxford University Press.

Jacob, M. (1994). Toward a methodological critique of sustainable development. *Journal of Developing Areas, 28,* 237–252.

Katzarov, B. (1964). *The theory of nationalisation.* Springer.

Keynes, J. M. (2012). *The economic consequences of peace.* CreateSpace Independent Publishing Platform.

Keynes, J. M. (2016). *The general theory of employment, interest and money.* Harcourt, Brace and World.

Kothari, I. V. (2005). *In from colonial administration to development studies: A postcolonial critique of the history of development studies. A radical history of development studies.* Zed Books.

Lanoszka, A. (2018). *International development: Socio-economic theories, legacies and strategies.* Routledge.

League of Nations commercial policy in the inter-wars period: International proposals and national policies (1942). https://searchworks.stanford.edu/view/1848548

Ledgerwood, J. Microfinance handbook: An institutional and financial perspective (Latest edition). World Bank.

Lewis, R. Grenada: A testing ground for Lewis' balanced development perspectives. Journal of Social and Economic Studies, 54, 206.

Lewis, W. A. (Sir). (1955). *The theory of economic growth.* Richard Irwin Inc.

MacDermot, N. (1981). *Speech delivered at the conference on development, human rights and the rule of law,* The Hague, The Report. https://archive.org/details/developmenthuman0000unse

Mader, P. (2015). *The political economy of microfinance: financializing poverty.* Palgrave Macmillan.

McNamara, R. S. (1970). The true dimension of the task. *International Development Review,* 5–6.

Mitrany, D. (1945). The functional approach to world organization. *International Affairs, 24*(3).

Mitrany, D. (1975). *A political theory for the new society in functionalism.* AJR Groom and P Taylor. University of London Press.

Momsen, J. H. (2004). *Gender and developments.* Routledge.

Moore, M. P., & Wickramasinghe, G. (1980). *Agriculture and society in the low country.* Agrarian Research and Training Institute.

North, D. (2005). *Understanding the process of economic change.* Princeton University Press.

Nussbaum, M. C. (2001). *Women and human development – The capabilities approach.* Cambridge University Press.

Odell, K. (2010). *Measuring the impact of microfinance: Taking another look.* Grameen Foundation.

Ormrod, J. E. (1995). *Human learning.* Prentice Hall.

Prebische, R. (1950). *The economic development of Latin America and its principal problems.* United Nations.

Rist, G. (2002). *History of development: From western origins to global faith* (2nd ed.). Zed Books.

Rostow, W. W. (1960). *The stages of economic growth: A non-communist manifesto.* Cambridge University Press.

Sachs, W. (2001). *Introduction to the work entitled the development dictionary: A guide to knowledge and power.* Witwatersrand University Press; also Zed Books Ltd.

Schumpeter, J. (2017). *Theory of economic development.* Routledge.

Schwarzenberger, G. (1945). The most-favoured Nation standard in British State practice. *British Yearbook of International Law, 22.*

Schwarzenberger, G. (1966). *The principles and standards of international economic law* (Vol. 117). *Recueil des Cours,* The Hague Academy of International Law.

Seers, D. (1971). The total relationship. In D. Seers, & L. Joy (Eds.), *Development in a divided world.* Penguin Books.

Sen, A. (1997). *Development thinking at the beginning of the 21st century in economic and social development in the XXI century.* Inter-American Development Bank and Johns Hopkins University Press.

Sen, A. (1999). *Development as freedom.* Random House.

Shapiro, J. China's environmental challenges (Latest edition). Polity Press.

Singer, H. W., & Ansari, J. A. (1977). *Rich and poor countries.* Allen and Unwin.

The Pearson Report. (1970, February). *Partners in development – The Pearson Report – A new strategy for development.* UNESCO Courier.

Tignor, R. L. W. (2005). *Arthur and the birth of development economics.* Princeton University Press.

Todaro, M. P., & Smith, S. C. (2015). *Economic development.* Pearson Publishers.

Turnbull, C. (1973). *The Mountain people.* Pan Books.

UN. (1962). *The UN development decade: Proposals for action.* UN.

UN Committee on. (1973). *Transnational corporations in world development transnational corporations.*

UNCTAD. (1985). *Draft code of conduct on transfer of technology.* https://digitallibrary.un.org/record/86199?v=pdf

UNDP Human development report 2016. Human Development for Everyone, New York, UNDP.

UNDP. (2014–2017). *The future we want: Rights and empowerment.* UNDP Gender Equality Strategy.

UNRISD. (1979). *An approach to development research.* https://digitallibrary.un.org/record/90664

UNRISD. (1980). *The quest for a united approach to development.* https://digitallibrary.un.org/record/95912

Wiesner, S., & Quinn, D. (2010). *Can 'bad' microfinance practices be the consequences of too much funding chasing too few microfinance institutions?* Discussion Paper 1 No. 2 ADA, Luxembourg.

Wilcox, C. A. A. (1949). *Charter of world trade.* Macmillan.

World Bank. (2015). *Does microfinance still hold promise for reaching the poor?* https://www.worldbank.org/en/news/feature/2015/03/30/does-microfinance-still-hold-promise-for-reaching-the-poor

World Bank. (2016). *South Sudan overview.* https://www.worldbank.org/en/country/southsudan/overview

World Bank Institute. (2009, June). *The capacity development research framework: A strategic and results-oriented approach to learning for capacity development.* https://documents1.worldbank.org/curated/en/482971468188374127/pdf/80632-WP-Capacity-Development-and-Results-Framework-Box-377295B-PUBLIC.pdf

Yergin, D., & Stanislaw, J. (2002). *The commanding heights – The battle for the world economy.* Simon and Schuster.

Yochi, M. The political element in the works of W Arthur Lewis: The 1954 model and African development. Developing Economics, XLIV(3), 339.

Yunus, M. (1998). *Banker to the poor: The story of the Grameen Bank.* Aurum Press.

Index

Printed in the USA
CPSIA information can be obtained
at www.ICGtesting.com
JSHW050042231124
74143JS00004B/76

9 781836 080657